Happy Trails!

The Road Less Traveled

TURNING YOUR RETIREMENT WORRIES INTO AN EXCURSION OF A LIFETIME

Mark Fricks

This document discusses general concepts for retirement planning, and is not intended to provide tax or legal advice. Individuals are urged to consult with their tax and legal professionals regarding these issues. This handbook should ensure that clients understand a) that annuities and some of their features have costs associated with them; b) that income received from annuities is taxable; and c) that annuities used to fund IRAs do not afford any additional measure of tax deferral for the IRA owner.

First Printing, 2015

Gradient Positioning Systems, LLC
4105 Lexington Avenue North, Suite 110
Arden Hills, MN 55126 (877) 901-0894

Contributors: Nick Stovall, Nate Lucius, Mike Binger and Gradient Positioning Systems, LLC.

Gradient Positioning Systems, LLC and Mark Fricks are not affiliated with or endorsed by the Social Security Administration or any government agency.

Acknowledgements

To my wife, Karen:
   who never gave up on me.

To my three children, Evan, Alyse and Anna:
   for your unconditional love.

To my friends:
   for your ability to laugh at my jokes as if they are funny.

To my clients:
   for trusting me and inspiring me to continue the good fight.

Table of Contents

Introduction

My aha moment came in the late fall of 2008 when I was sitting across from a dear old lady in her late 70s whom we'll call Irene. Now Irene was a widow living off the fixed income of her retirement nest egg, and she came to see me about the loss her account had just sustained. Many retirees lost a great deal of money after the stock market downturn of 2008, and I was telling Irene that actually, we had done a pretty good job for her. Based on the way the firm I was working for at the time operated, I launched into my explanation about how most people lost an average of 30 percent, and Irene only lost 17 percent, so really, she came out ahead of most people and should feel pretty good. And as I was explaining this to her, I saw the look on her face and it hit me: she just lost $90,000 of her hard-earned money and here I was telling her that she should feel good. Ninety-thousand dollars at the age of 70 that she would never be able to get back again because Irene's working days were over. She sat across from me, this little old

1

lady, and I realized, we're missing something here. There's got to be more to retirement planning!

I went back to the drawing board after that day, researching, reading, attending conferences and interviewing other advisors. I had been following all the rules but what I realized was that the rules had something missing. Over the course of the next two years, I developed my own firm—MasterPlan Retirement Consultants—and protecting assets and creating income for pre- and post-retirees became my number one goal.

Irene was right to be worried on the day she came to talk to me. She passed away at the age of 82 without a penny to her name. Part of this was because her money had been left in buy and hold stock market investments; the other part was due to health care expenses. Irene's daughter, Katie, retired this year in her early 60s and she is now one of my biggest advocates. She has seen both sides of the coin—what happens when you don't protect your assets, and what happens when you do. Katie is enjoying a very different retirement than the one had by her mother.

NOT YOUR FATHER'S STOCK MARKET

In the 1950s, the common man or woman down the street wasn't investing in the stock market. In the early 1980s not long after Congress created the Individual Retirement Account (IRA), followed soon thereafter by the 401(k), I walked into my first big corporate job. I was filling out the paperwork and the woman from the Human Resource department said to me, "You qualify for a 401(k) retirement account."

I said, "Great. What's that?"

They told me I could start putting some money into the stock market. I had no idea which stocks to choose. "Just pick some," they told me. "Pick the ones that did the best last year." So I did that, and I came to learn that was a bit like driving using a rearview mirror only. But still, back then, everybody did okay. In the 1990s, we were zooming around in the stock market and everything was hunky-dory until the market shifted and we took a few big hits. That changed everybody's lives. Nobody saw the market downturn of 2008 coming and people are still talking about it today, wondering what the heck happened? That really woke a lot of people up to the realization that the stock market today is not the stock market of yesteryear.

As a nation, we have gotten pretty callous to the idea of risk. Going backwards in time again, if you take a look at Vegas in the 1950s and 1960s, you'd see it was filled with gangsters and mobsters and what people did there was called gambling. Today, people take their families to Vegas and we don't call it gambling, we call it gaming. In the same way that Vegas is a different place than it used to be, so, too, is the stock market. Things in the marketplace have gotten a lot more volatile because we have become a global economy. You can have the best money manager in the world, but if a bomb goes off in Sri Lanka or if China has an economic problem, it definitely affects our economy in ways that it never did 20 years ago.

The bottom line here is that it's impossible these days to predict what the market will do. You can't manage returns. But you CAN manage risk.

MOUNTAIN CLIMBING AND YOUR RETIREMENT YEARS

Sir Edmund Hilary is crowned with the achievement of being the first climber to reach the peak of Mt. Everest. What's significant, however, is that, based on current research, he may not have been the first person to reach the top of Everest. He was the first person *to make it all the way up and then back down again* still alive and in one piece. Thirty years earlier, a man by the name of Mallory hired his friend, Irvin, to help him get to the top of Mt. Everest.

3

Mallory was credited as being one of the most experienced climbers in the world at the time and his friend Irvin was also a good climber in excellent physical condition. Together they did manage to top the highest peak in the world, but they never made it back down. Why? Because as with so many things in life, *getting down can be, and most often is, the most difficult part of the journey.*

Retirement is like reaching the summit of a great mountain. You put a great deal of time, effort and planning into reaching the pinnacle, but not as much time, effort and planning into making the trip back down. This sheds light on how people need to make an adjustment to their assets. The same strategies, tools and philosophies used to get UP the mountain are completely different as you head DOWN. You're tired, for one thing, and your health isn't as good. Your equipment is worn out, you might have lost a few items, and the food you have with you has to last all the way until you get to base camp. There is no longer the reward of a stunning summit—you're just trying to stay alive. You've got to switch gears and enter into a new and different phase.

Going up the mountain of life is like the accumulation phase of our financial life. Your focus is on how much money you can put away and how much your employer can match. Every year you adjust and try to save a bit more or get a higher return. When you finally get to the top, you are at the peak of your earning potential, and now you've got to go back down the mountain schlepping all your stuff. You have to carry the weight of inflation, taxes and the fear of outliving your money, just to name a few. Going back down the mountain you enter into a new phase, the "de-accumulation" phase. Your focus now should be on preserving what assets you have. The health, safety and enjoyment of your retirement years depend on it.

WHAT DOES YOUR RETIREMENT LOOK LIKE?

At MasterPlan Retirement Consultants, we spend a lot of time talking about your retirement roadmap because virtually no one who comes to see us has a plan for getting back down the mountain. You might have pieces—investments products you bought, contributions you made together with a wish list. But there's no plan.

People often confuse investments products with plans. They think their 401(k) is a retirement plan when in reality, it is only a product. A 401(k) and an IRA can be compared to the materials you need to build a car. They are like the wheels or windows or maybe the steering wheel, but you can't make it very far down the road with car parts alone. You've got to put all those components together into a cohesive whole, so all the parts work together to help you get to where you want to go.

I think of a retirement plan as your roadmap because it contains not just the directions, but all the cool things and places you want to do and see along the way. It plans for visits to see your family or a destination like The Giant Ball of String, and takes care of basic necessities like meals and lodging. This can be compared to your retirement income because we all know that travel is no fun when you're uncomfortable, tired, and hungry. A retirement plan needs to start with your basic, most essential needs but it must also take into consideration your preferences and health concerns. A good plan also accounts for risk, or the things that can go wrong. Your roadmap for retirement must include the following to ensure the safety and longevity of your trip:

- *Where do you want to go?* Your goals, desires and purpose during your retirement years.
- *Risk and the magic underwear.* What kinds of investments should you pack? Is the stock market right for you during retirement? Chapter two includes the rollicking story of Chuck and the magic underwear.

- *Junk Food While Driving*: It might come in pretty wrappers, but not all investments are designed to do the same thing. Some are good for you and some aren't so good during retirement. You want a steady supply of good, reliable fuel. Chapter three is about The Colors of Money.
- *How to keep fuel in the tank*: A chapter about your basic needs—income planning.
- *Getting as much as you can*: Social Security maximization and your benefit.
- *What if I need more gas?* How to write your own pension plan to fill the income gap.
- *Taking the long way*: Streamlining your tax liabilities is like making sure you don't waste gas. You make more money by saving on taxes than you do by earning more money. Chapter 10 is about tax planning.
- *Who do you want to remember?* Creating a lasting legacy is about more than just filling out the correct paperwork—it requires collaboration between your intentions and the legal documents in order to avoid probate, disinheritance and tax penalties.
- *Don't be afraid to ask for directions*: Getting advice from a knowledgeable financial professional can make all the difference between a trip that is fun and enjoyable and one that ends in disaster. Enjoy the peace of mind that comes from working with a professional who has your best interests at heart.

The information you've read in this introduction may have already changed your view on retirement. The information in the ensuing chapters can change your approach to life in retirement by giving you confidence, knowledge, and most importantly, control over your retirement.

This book will address your entire financial situation from four perspectives:
- Income
- Asset accumulation
- Taxes
- Legacy

YOUR RETIREMENT SHERPA

Going back to our mountain climbing analogy, what did Sir Edmund Hillary have that Mallory didn't have? The answer has been long speculated by climbers and non-climbers alike, but one of the most noted differences is the fact that Hillary didn't take a friend climbing with him. Hillary hired a Sherpa by the name of Tenzing Norgay. Sherpas are native to the Himalayan mountain region, naturally acclimated to the higher altitudes and able to climb with heavy gear on their back. Because of their knowledge, skill and familiarity with severe weather patterns, they are hired to guide climbers safely up and down the mountain. A Sherpa, in short, is a professional.

At MasterPlan Retirement Consultants we take the job of guiding your retirement to heart. We don't just want you to get back down the mountain; we want you to enjoy the journey along the way. You've worked and saved your entire life so that the enjoyment of these de-accumulation years would come easy. Let us assist you with the burden of asset allocation, tax liabilities and the logistics of leaving behind a legacy. *We'll be your Sherpa.*

We are a full-service boutique firm that specializes in handling all three aspects of retirement risk including money management, tax strategies and estate planning. Our estate attorney, tax attorney, mortgage people and Medicare/Medicaid specialists are there to make sure that all the areas that can cause risk to your retirement years are planned for and addressed so that you can rest easy with peace of mind. As an investment advisor with over 26 years of experience in financial services, we never take on more clients than we can comfortably handle. We keep our firm relatively small to make sure that we have your back covered, and we make sure that no one ever gets lost coming back down the mountain.

Mark Fricks, Investment Advisor Representative, Registered Financial Consultant and Chartered Retirement Planning Counselor, founder of MasterPlan Retirement Consultants, DBA of Fricks and Associates, Inc., and MasterPlan Wealth Advisors, a Registered Investment Advisor firm.

1

Destination Retirement

Are we there yet?

Jack and Beverly are age 67 and 65 respectively and they live in the red clay state of Georgia. They have decided they would like to go to California and so they walk out of their house, get into their car and head west. George has his wallet and Beverly has her purse, so they have cash and access to money. But other than that, they don't bring a map or supplies and they don't even pack a suitcase. They just get into the car and point west.

They hope that if they just keep driving, eventually they'll get to California. Their thinking is that as long as they head west they should eventually get there. Right?

While Jack and Beverly might sound like a couple of eighteen year-old renegades, a lot of people approach retirement the exact same way. They take their money, get into the car and drive. They *hope* they have enough money and they *hope* they will get to where they want to go. But most people don't really have a plan.

The key word in that sentiment and the word that can make retirement feel like a looming problem instead of a rewarding life stage, is *hope*. You hope you'll have enough money. You hope nothing will go wrong. You hope you'll make it okay. Only with retirement, the stakes are much higher than just a fun trip to a new place. Your money has to last longer than the time it takes to get to California. Your assets, the wealth you have worked so hard to accumulate during all your working years, have to last the rest of your life. Retirement isn't just a lark. *It's an excursion of a lifetime.*

Leaving your retirement up to chance is unadvisable by nearly any standard, yet millions of people find themselves *hoping* instead of planning for a happy ending. With information, tools and professional guidance, creating a successful retirement plan can put you in the driver's seat of your financial management. It's often been said that people spend more time planning for their vacations then they do for their retirement years, so we're going to take a light-hearted approach. We're going to look at your retirement as the excursion of a lifetime, and we're going to plan for it just as you would any other exciting and wonderful vacation.

WHAT TO THINK ABOUT BEFORE THE TRIP

When you plan for a trip, one of the first things you do is figure out what you want to do and see, both along the way and when you get there. The same thing applies to your retirement years. We often get so caught up in the worry of money, we forget that the reason we saved in the first place is so that we can enjoy ourselves. What do you want to do during retirement? What are your dreams, goals and issues? Who do you want to see? And where have you been planning to visit?

The foundation of a retirement plan starts with what you want to do and how you want to do it. We talk about hobbies, activities and events. Do you like to take the back roads? Are you in a hurry to get there? Are you value-oriented and only looking for the cheap hotels? Or do you own an RV? We talk about who you are and what you want to do. We also ask about the people who are important to you. We ask about family because the people who are important to you have to be included in your plan.

Think of it this way: when you go on a trip and rent a car, do you show up at the rental agency and take whatever shiny thing on wheels is available? A three-wheeled scooter? A two-door hatchback? A minivan with dog hair on the seats and a broken air conditioner?

Or do you think about your trip and ask yourself a few questions such as: how many people will be traveling in the car? How many hours will we be riding together each day? How many miles will we be going? What kind of terrain will we encounter? Getting the right vehicle doesn't cost any more than just showing up and taking whatever is available on the lot. Getting the right vehicle also means everyone going on the trip will be taken care of and be a lot more comfortable. But the biggest upside is that you will all have a greater chance of getting exactly where you want to go.

Your retirement vehicle can be compared to the organization and structuring of your assets. We want your money to be able to provide for the people who are most important to you. When we talk about your retirement plan we ask you questions such as:

- Do you want to help your grandkids pay for college?
- Are you taking care of an elder parent?
- Do you have any family nearby?

Your roadmap to retirement starts with a conversation about you and your life. These questions may sound personal, but money is personal. Money represents more than the paper it's printed on. It is the embodiment of your time, your talents, and your commitments. It buys the food you eat, the house you sleep in, the car you drive, and the clothes you wear. It also helps provide you with the lifestyle you want to live once you retire.

THE DIFFERENCE BETWEEN A GOAL AND A DREAM

When you are eighteen and young with decades of living ahead of you, there is nothing wrong with getting in a car and just driving away. Maybe you've done this yourself: gone on a trip with only a wallet and a dream. There's nothing wrong with that, if you have the time. For most people entering into retirement, they don't have the time to drive for days on end in the wrong direction. Doing that jeopardizes the entire trip because they might run out of gas, run out money, or worse, run out of time. When you enter into retirement you are no longer eighteen and that's why a plan becomes so important.

A plan is different from a dream. A dream gives you direction, vision and a warm fuzzy feeling. But a dream alone doesn't get things done. When you take the time to plan, you recast that dream as a goal. A goal is a specific and written plan with directions that tell you how to get there.

> » *Bob and Vivian came into the office to talk about their retirement assets. But Vivian wasn't talking to Bob and Bob wasn't talking to Vivian. They were both upset, each for his/her own reasons. Vivian was tired of Bob managing her life like he used to manage his business. Bob was tired of having to ask permission before he went golfing and he didn't want to wash any more dishes. Bob and Vivian were retired, but they didn't know what to do with their new-found time. Most importantly, they didn't know what to do together.*

RECLAMATION DAY: RETIRE WITH A PURPOSE

The word *retirement* has many negative connotations and quite frankly is a terrible word for today's generation of Boomers. They're not fading away, withdrawing from society, or sitting in rocking chairs whittling on the porch. At 65, they are vibrant, healthy individuals who still have a lot left to give. Given the average life expectancy these days, most people can count on living another 20 years past the age of 65.* Even estimating on the low side, ten years is a good chunk of time. What do you want to do with those years? What is your passion? What do you want these years to be all about?

Talking about *the purpose* of your retirement years is another (surprising!) conversation that needs to happen before we get down to money matters. This is especially important for married couples who in many cases are spending greater amounts of time together than they have spent in a long time. Without the distraction of work, kids and career, what will you do with your time?

Chances are you gave up a lot of the things you really enjoyed doing during your working years. Maybe it's time to start adding those things back into your life. Reclamation is a restoration of usefulness and productivity. What do you want to do? Do you have a garage in the backyard where you want to work on cars or radios? Do you want to start a business or build an art studio? Join a book club or a bowling league? Now is the time to ask yourself, what's next? What thrills you? What do you want to do? What are your hobbies and skills? What do you care about? Who do you want to help? Maybe it's traveling with a purpose and volunteering in other countries; maybe it's reading to children at your grandson's elementary school. Whatever it is, chances are you have talents just waiting to be put to use. Your retirement

---

*http://www.ncbi.nlm.nih.gov/books/NBK62373/

plan should include the methods and strategies to reclaim those talents and put those activities and interests back into your life.

WHERE YOU ARE NOW

You have spent a lifetime earning, spending, and hopefully, accumulating money. When the time comes for retirement, you want your money to provide you with a comfortable lifestyle and stable income after your working days are done. You might also have other desires, such as traveling, purchasing property, or moving to be closer to your family (or farther away.) You may also want your assets to provide for your loved ones after you are gone.

The truth is that it takes more than just money to fulfill those needs and desires. It takes a comprehensive plan that considers all the working parts of your complicated or not-so-complicated life. That's why we start with questions about you, who you are, and the people close to you. All of this directly influences the choices we make when organizing and planning for money management strategies. As you start thinking about retirement and planning for all the things you want to do, you'll find a reoccurring theme often pops up: *the fear of running out of money.*

While you may have built up a 401(k), an IRA, and Social Security benefits, do you know what your financial picture really looks like? Do you know how much money you need to pay the everyday bills? Do you know how many guaranteed sources of income you'll have during your retirement years?

After identifying your goal or destination, your next step is to figure out where you are now with regards to your finances. How can you plan a route if you don't know your starting point? As they say in Georgia, *that dog won't hunt.* If you plan a route from a different location on the map other than where you are currently located, your future will be full of wrong turns.

It's time to look at all your investments: annuities, life insurance plans and 401(k)s; IRAs, money market accounts and any savings. We'll also look at past tax returns to get an idea of income and tax liability. We'll see what needs to be fixed, tweaked or changed in order to keep your investments in line with your goals.

Often times we find investment vehicles that overlap and cost money you don't need to be spending. For example, you might be paying for an income rider without ever turning on the income portion of the product. This is a lot like driving around in an RV and still paying for a Bed and Breakfast suite at the end of the day. You either want to sell the RV or stop paying for the Bed and Breakfast. At the very least, you want to know about the investment products you own to identify what they are actually doing for you and what you would like them to do for you. Structuring assets to create an income-generating retirement requires a different approach than earning income via the workforce. Add the complexities of taxes, required minimum distributions (RMDs) from IRAs and legacy planning, and you can begin to see why happy endings require more than hope. They need a focused and well-executed plan.

THE IMPORTANCE OF A PLANFUL APPROACH

The way you approach your retirement impacts your income, the taxes your assets are subject to, your financial stability in the future, and your legacy. It is a truism among financial professionals that *one hour of organizing your assets can be worth more than an entire lifetime of working and saving* when it comes to retirement. Why is this so?

The fact of the matter is that after working and saving for a lifetime, entering retirement changes all of the rules you have known and followed for your entire career. Instead of an earning and saving paradigm, you are moving into an income and asset leveraging paradigm where you need to use the money you have earned and saved to generate income and preserve your assets for you. Making sure your assets last for your lifetime will depend on how you decide to invest them, and in what order you will spend them

Advice about what to do with money has been around as long as money has existed. Hindsight allows us to see which advice was good and which advice didn't cut the mustard. Some sources of advice have been around for a very long time. While there are some basic investment concepts that have stood the test of time, most strategies that work adapt to changing conditions in the market, in the economy and the world, as well as changes in your personal circumstances.

The reality is that investment strategies and savings plans that worked in the past have encountered challenging new circumstances that have turned them on their heads. The market downturn in the early 2000's, along with the "Great Recession" of 2007-2008 highlighted how old investment ideas were not only ineffective but incredibly destructive to the retirement plans of millions of Americans. The dawn of an entirely restructured health care system brings with it new options and challenges that will undoubtedly change the way insurance companies provide investment products and services.

Perhaps the most important lessons investors learned from the past decade is that not understanding where your money is invested (and the potential risks of those investments) can work against you, your plans for retirement and your legacy. Saving and investing money isn't enough to truly get the most out of it. You must have a planful approach to managing your assets.

Essentially, managing your money and your investments is an ongoing process that requires customization and adaptation to a changing world. And make no mistake; the world is always changing. What worked for your parents or even your parents' parents was probably good advice back then. People in retirement or approaching retirement today need new ideas and professional guidance.

A MAP IS NOT A PLAN

Before we continue on our journey, it's important to take a minute and address the flaw in our analogy. A map can't plan your retirement any more than a pill can make you healthy. Your retirement roadmap is like a prescription you follow and as such it must be constantly updated. An excursion of this length isn't something you plan for once and then forget about. A plan of this magnitude has to be adjusted, tweaked and looked at often because as you go along, the things, people and circumstances of your life change. Figuring out how to get from point A to point B is just one part of the process. There are many more complications.

A map doesn't tell you what to do if you get tired, lost or confused. It doesn't tell you what to see, what to do or where to eat. It's what you need to get started on the trip, but what do you need to keep going? In other words, how do you make sure that the fuel in the tank is enough to last the whole way and what if the car breaks down? As this translates to your retirement concerns, you might ask, should I be worried about growing my assets? Is the stock market the right place for my money during retirement? Most people don't realize all the complications involved in retirement planning until they get ready to retire and they start looking at it. Our next chapter deals with the realities of stock market risk.

CHAPTER 1 RECAP //

- Just like planning for a vacation or a trip, your retirement plan needs to consider your goals and objectives, or it won't be a good plan for you. The answers to the question, *when should I retire*, will be different for everyone, based on your lifestyle and the people in it who are important to you.

- There is a difference between a retirement product such as a mutual fund or annuity and a retirement plan. As you move out of the working stage of your life, you are no longer earning income. A shift must be made from the accumulation of your money to the management of your money. Before you take off on your retirement trip, identify where you are now by taking the time to understand what you are invested in and what those investments are doing for you.

- The rules for retirement planning have changed. Investing the way your parents did will not pay off and the majority of investment ideas used by financial professionals in the 1990s aren't applicable to today's markets. That kind of investing will likely get you in trouble and compromise your retirement. Today, you need a better PLAN. Having a planful approach to retirement gives consideration to today's stock market and economy, and the individual concerns of you, the investor.

2

What the Heck Just Happened?
Stock Market Risk and Your Retirement

"The U.S. has developed a new weapon that destroys people but leaves buildings standing. It's called the stock market."
- Jay Leno

The stock market has long been relied upon to grow money. During retirement, growth is an important part of asset management and one solution to the dilemma of running out of money. But with growth comes risk. How much risk depends on the percentage of your investments connected to stock market volatility.

We talked at the beginning of the book about how as a culture, our perception of risk has shifted over the years. People these days are so comfortable with gambling that they now call it gaming;

so too it follows that a lot of people don't mind with having the majority of their retirement nest egg sitting in the stock market. The sudden market downturn of 2008 shattered that illusion of safety, when the average investor lost 30 percent of the money saved in their 401(k) plans. A lot can be said for those cautionary tales of woe. The following story isn't about stock market loss but rather about the power of illusion. When it comes to our assets, we need to perceive risk correctly. The safety of our retirement depends on it.

We call this story, Chuck and the Magic Underwear.

» *As a key contributor to the marketing of Mazola Canola Oil, Chuck went on a business trip to New Orleans. He had a trailer with a big banner and a grill, and he spent the day frying up food and handing out free samples to the crowd gathered for the festival. It was a hot, humid, miserable day and Chuck was out in the elements from nine that morning until seven that night. By the time he got back to his hotel room, he was sunburned, sweaty and chafed in places too terrible to mention. He got undressed, showered and laid down on the bed for some much deserved rest.*

The next day, Chuck was charged with the task of doing it all over again on another hot and humid day. He couldn't bear the thought of underwear so, much as it made him uncomfortable, he decided to go commando. Chuck was a bit on the modest side, however, and so he grabbed a clean pair of underwear just in case and tucked them in his pocket.

At the end of another arduous, hot day, Chuck was walking back to his hotel room to have dinner. He passed along Bourbon Street to find it crowded with more happy people than he had ever seen in his entire life. He was so struck by the crowds he slowed down just as a group of eight, beautiful women approached.

They were dressed to the nines, gorgeous women, out for a night on the town to celebrate their friend's bachelorette party. In high spirits, they started talking to Chuck and explaining how they were actually on a scavenger hunt. "We have to get all ten items on our list before we can meet back up at the bar." The bride-to-be turned around and taped to her back was a list of ten items. Item number one read: a pair of men's underwear.

Now Chuck was a modest fellow who harbored secret ambitions. He'd gone to his share of magic shows. With a gleam in his eyes he said, "Well now, ladies, I think I can help you out here." They all giggled and started to take him inside to the nearest establishment where he could change, but Chuck had something else in mind. He stood his ground right there on the sidewalk among the crowd and said, "Oh no, ladies. I'll just give them to you right here."

This was met with hooting and much laughter.

With a flourish Chuck turned his back to the gathering crowd.

The women held their breath and passersbys stopped to watch. Chuck wriggled and writhed and performed fake 'taking off underwear' moves. Then, at just the right moment, he slipped the clean trunks from out of his pocket, turned around and said, "Ta-da!"

He twirled the underwear on his finger. The ladies gasped in amazement. And like any good magician, Chuck never revealed his trick.

That night the women on Bourbon Street were left wondering *what the heck just happened?* The same kind of thing left thousands of pre- and post-retirees in a different kind of stupor after the market downturn of 2008. Just prior to '06 and '07, people were feeling great and out having a good time. The market crash came and people were left feeling naked. Most people never saw it coming. Others wondered if they would ever be able to retire. It was like Chuck and the magic underwear: they wanted to know—what the heck just happened?

WHAT MARKET LOSS MEANS TO MOST RETIREES

Taking a hit in the market hurts, especially when the security of your retirement income is connected to that loss. People are left wondering what happened, wondering if they can retire and wondering if there is a cure. The very real but sad truth about stock market loss is that once the money is gone, it's gone. There is no magic underwear when it comes to losing money. The only trick is time and in most cases, it takes another six to eight years to grow that money back again. Most people don't have that kind of time once they enter into retirement because they need to rely on that money for their income.

You might have the sentiment, "the market always comes back," but even if you do get back to where you were before the loss, your money isn't growing and earning the same way it was before the hit occurred. The *math of rebounds*, as it is known, uses the percentage of the investment, and not the dollar amount, to calculate what you will need to earn in order to recapture your loses.

For example, if you had $100,000 invested in the stock market in 2007, and along came the downturn of 2008, the market took a reduction of 50 percent. So then your $100,000 would have become $50,000. What would have to happen for you to get back up to $100,000? It took a 50 percent loss to lose $50,000 but it would take a 100-percent gain to get your account back to where you were before. What this means for the average retiree is that it takes a LONG time to dig out of the hole.

EMOTIONS AND INVESTING

The most important thing to remember as you consider the allocation of your retirement funds is that times have changed and this is not your father's stock market. We are now tied to a global economy. The exponential rise in technology means over 75 to 76 percent of trades are done by computer.* Stocks trade in a matter of nanoseconds in a climate where one false tweet can cause the market to plummet.** The market is experiencing huge ups and downs based on events that may or may not be true and in the middle of this, we have Ma and Pa Kettle waiting to retire. They ride alone on this train-ride roller coaster and who knows where they are going to end up?

When you are managing your money by yourself, emotions inevitably enter into the mix. The Dow Jones Industrial Average and the S&P 500 represent more to you than market fluctuations. They represent a portion of your retirement. It's hard not to be emotional about it.

Everyone knows you should buy low and sell high. But this is what is more likely to happen:

The market takes a downturn, similar to the 2008 crash, and investors see as much as a 30 percent loss in their stock holdings. It's hard to watch, and it's harder to bear the pain of losing that much money. The math of rebounds means that they will need to rely on even larger gains just to get back to where things were before the downturn. They sell. But eventually, and inevitably, the market begins to rise again. Maybe slowly, maybe with some moderate growth, but by the time the average investor notices an upward trend and wants to buy in again, they have already missed

---

*http://money.cnn.com/2013/07/08/investing/stock-market-citadel/index.html
**http://business.time.com/2013/04/24/how-does-one-fake-tweet-cause-a-stock-market-crash/

a great deal of the gains. Cynthia's situation illustrates how market volatility can have major repercussions for an individual investor.

> » *Cynthia has worked for the Papadilla Spear advertising company for 34 years. During her time there, she acquires bonuses and pay raises that often include shares of stock in the company. She also dedicates part of her paycheck every month to a 401(k) that bought Papadilla Spear stock. By the time she retires, Cynthia has $250,000 worth of company stock.*
>
> *Although she had contributed to her 401(k) account every month, Cynthia doesn't cultivate any other assets that could generate income for her during retirement. Cynthia also retires early at age 62 because of her failing health. The commute to work every day was becoming difficult in her weakened condition and she wanted to enjoy the rest of her life in retirement instead of working at Papadilla Spear.*
>
> *Because she retires early, Cynthia fails to maximize her Social Security benefit. While she lives a modest lifestyle, her income needs will still be $3,500 per month. Cynthia's monthly Social Security check will only cover $1,900, leaving her with a $1,600 income gap. To supplement her Social Security check, Cynthia sells $1,600 of her company stock each month to meet her income needs. A $250,000 401(k) is nothing to sneeze at, but reducing its value by $1,600 every month will barely last Cynthia 10 years. And that's if the market stays neutral or grows modestly. If the market takes a downturn, the money that Cynthia relied on to fill her income gap will rapidly diminish. Even if the market starts going up in a couple of years, it will take much larger gains for her to recover the value that she lost.*
>
> *Unhappily for Cynthia, she retired in 2007, just before the major market downturn that lasted for several years. She lost more than 20 percent of the value of her stock. Because*

Cynthia needed to sell her stock to meet her basic income needs, the market price of the stock was secondary to her need for the money. When she needed money, she was forced to sell however many shares she needed to fill her income gap that month. And if she has a financial crisis, involving her need for medical care, for example, she will be forced to sell stock even if the market is low and her shares are nearly worthless.

Cynthia did not realize that she could have relied on an investment structured to deliver her a regular income while protecting the value of her investment. She could have kept her $250,000 from diminishing while enjoying her lifestyle into retirement regardless of the volatility of the market. Ideally, Cynthia would have restructured her 401(k) to reflect the level of risk that she was able to take.

In 2013, DALBAR, the well-respected financial services market research firm, released their annual "Quantitative Analysis of Investment Behavior" report (QAIB). The report studied the impact of market volatility on individual investors: people like Cynthia, or anyone who was managing (or mismanaging) their own investments in the stock market.

According to the study, volatility not only caused investors to make decisions based on their emotions, those decisions also harmed their investments and prevented them from realizing potential gains. So why do people meddle so much with their investments when the market is fluctuating? Part of the reason is that many people have financial obligations that they don't have control over. Significant expenses like house payments, the unexpected cost of replacing a broken-down car, and medical bills can put people in a position where they need money. If they need to sell investments to come up with that money, they don't have the luxury of selling when they *want* to. They must sell when they *need* to.

DALBAR's "Quantitative Analysis of Investor Behavior" has been used to measure the effects of investors' buying, selling and mutual fund switching decisions since 1994. The QAIB shows time and time again over nearly a 20 year period that the average investor earns less, and in many cases, significantly less than the performance of mutual funds suggests. QAIB's goal is to improve independent investor performance and to help financial professionals provide helpful advice and investment strategies that address the concerns and behaviors of the average investor.

An excerpt from the report claims that:*

"QAIB offers guidance on how and where investor behaviors can be improved. No matter what the state of the mutual fund industry, boom or bust: Investment results are more dependent on investor behavior than on fund performance. Mutual fund investors who hold on to their investments are more successful than those who time the market.

QAIB uses data from the Investment Company Institute (ICI), Standard & Poor's and Barclays Capital Index Products to compare mutual fund investor returns to an appropriate set of benchmarks.

There are actually three primary causes for the chronic shortfall for both equity and fixed income investors:

1. *Capital not available to invest. This accounts for 25 percent to 35 percent of the shortfall.*
2. *Capital needed for other purposes. This accounts for 35 percent to 45 percent of the shortfall.*
3. *Psychological factors. These account for 45 percent to 55 percent of the shortfall."*

---

*2013 QAIB, Dalbar, March 2013

The key findings of Dalbar's QAIB report provide compelling statistics about how individual investment strategies produced negative outcomes for the majority of investors:

- Psychological factors account for 45 percent to 55 percent of the chronic investment return shortfall for both equity and fixed income investors.

- Asset allocation is designed to handle the investment decision-making for the investor, which can materially reduce the shortfall due to psychological factors.

- Successful asset allocation investing requires investors to act on two critical imperatives:
  1. Balance capital preservation and appreciation so that they are aligned with the investor's objective.
  2. Select a qualified allocator.

- The best way for an investor to determine their risk tolerance is to utilize a risk tolerance assessment. However, these assessments must be accessible and usable.

- Evaluating allocator quality requires analysis of the allocator's underlying investments, decision making process and whether or not past efforts have produced successful outcomes.

- Choosing a top allocator makes a significant difference in the investment results one will achieve.

- Mutual fund retention rates suggest that the average investor has not remained invested for long enough periods to derive the potential benefits of the investment markets.

- Retention rates for asset allocation funds exceed those of equity and fixed income funds by over a year.

- Investors' ability to correctly time the market is highly dependent on the direction of the market. Investors generally guess right more often in up markets. However, in 2012 investors guessed right only 42 percent of the time during a bull market.

- Analysis of investor fund flows compared to market performance further supports the argument that investors are unsuccessful at timing the market. Market upswings rarely coincide with mutual fund inflows while market downturns do not coincide with mutual fund outflows.
- The shortfall in the long-term annualized return of the average mutual fund equity investor and the S&P 500 continued to decrease in 2012.
- The average fixed income investor has failed to keep up with inflation in nine out of the last 14 years.*

It doesn't take a financial services market research report to tell you that market volatility is out of your control. The report does prove, however, that before you experience market volatility, you should have an investment plan, and when the market is fluctuating, you should stand by your investment plan. You should also review and discuss your investment plan with your financial professional on a regular basis, ensuring he/she is aware of any changes in your goals, financial circumstances, your health or your risk tolerance. When the economy is under stress and the markets are volatile, investors can feel vulnerable. That vulnerability causes people to tinker with their portfolios in an attempt to outsmart the market. Financial professionals, however, don't try to time the market for their clients. They try to tap into the gains that can be realized by committing to long-term investment strategies.

HOPE SO VS. KNOW SO MONEY

Understanding how to manage your assets entails risk management, risk diversification, tax planning and income planning preparation throughout your life stages. These strategies can help

---

*2013 QAIB, Dalbar, March 2013

you leverage more from each one of the hard-earned dollars you set aside for your retirement. Let's take a look at some of the basic truths about money as it relates to saving for retirement. There are essentially two kinds of money: *Hope So Money* and *Know So*. Everyone can divide their money into these two categories. Some have more of one kind than the other. The goal isn't to eliminate one kind of money but to balance them as you approach retirement.

Hope So Money is money that is at risk. It fluctuates with the market. It has no minimum guarantee. It is subject to investor activity, stock prices, market trends, buying trends, etc. You

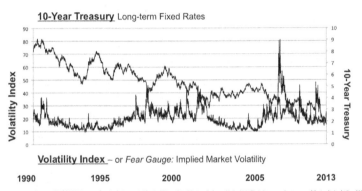

10-Year Treasury Long-term Fixed Rates

Volatility Index – or *Fear Gauge:* Implied Market Volatility

Source: Yahoo Finance – 12-31-2013. VIX is a trademarked ticker symbol for the Chicago Board Options Exchange Market Volatility Index, a popular measure of the implied volatility of S&P 500 index options. Often referred to as the fear index or the fear gauge, it represents one measure of the market's expectation of stock market volatility over the next 30 day period. (wikipedia.com) The CBOE 10-year Treasury Note (TNX) is based on 10 times the yield-to-maturity on the most recently auctioned 10-year Treasury note. Past performance does not guarantee future results. Some illustrations may show how a market index has performed. An investor cannot invest in an index, although there are some investments designed to mirror index performance. Past performance is not a guarantee of future results.

The VIX, or volatility index, of the market represents expected market volatility. When the VIX drops, economic experts expect less volatility. When the VIX rises, more volatility is expected.

1. *VIX is a trademarked ticker symbol for the Chicago Board Options Exchange (CBOE) Market Volatility Index, a popular measure of the implied volatility of S&P 500 index options. Often referred to as the fear index or the fear gauge, it represents one measure of the market's expectation of stock market volatility over the next 30 day period. (wikipedia.com)*

2. *The CBOE 10-Year Treasury Note (TNX) is based on 10 times the yield-to-maturity on the most recently auctioned 10-year Treasury note.*

get the picture. This money is exposed to more risk but also has the potential for more reward. Because the market is subject to change, you can't really be sure what the value of your investments will be worth in the future. You can't really *rely* on it at all. For this reason, we refer to it as Hope So Money. This doesn't mean you shouldn't have some money invested in the market, but it would be dangerous to assume you can know what it will be worth in the future.

Hope So Money is an important element of a retirement plan, especially in the early stages of planning when you can trade volatility for potential returns, and when a longer investment timeframe is available to you. In the long run, time can smooth out the ups and downs of money exposed to the market. Working with a professional and leveraging a long-term investment strategy has the potential to create rewarding returns from Hope So Money.

Know So Money, on the other hand, is safer when compared to Hope So Money. Know So Money is made up of dependable, low-risk or no-risk money, and investments that you can count on. Social Security is one of the most common forms of Know So Money. Income you draw or will draw from Social Security is guaranteed. You have paid into Social Security your entire career, and you can rely on that money during your retirement. Unlike the market, rates of growth for Know So Money are dependent on 10-year treasury rates. The 10-year treasury, or TNX, is commonly considered to represent a very secure and safe place for your money, hence Know So Money. The 10-year treasury drives key rates for things such as mortgage rates or CD rates. Know So Money may not be as exciting as Hope So Money, but it is safer. You can be fairly sure you will have it in the future.

Knowing the difference between Hope So and Know So Money is an important step towards a successful retirement plan. People who are 55 or older and who are looking ahead to retirement should be relying on more Know So Money than Hope So Money.

Ideally, the rates of return on Hope So and Know So Money would have an overlapping area that provided an acceptable rate of risk for both types of money. In the early 1990s, interest rates were high and market volatility was low. At that time, you could invest in either Hope So or Know So Money options because the rates of return were similar from both Know So and Hope So investments, and you were likely to be fairly successful with a wide range of investment options. At that time, you could expose yourself to an acceptable amount of risk or an acceptable fixed rate. Basically, it was difficult to make a mistake during that time period. Today, you don't have those options. Market volatility is at all-time highs while interest rates are at all-time lows. They are so far apart from each other that it is hard to know what to do with your money.

Yesterday's investment rules may not work today. Not only could they hamper achieving your goals, they may actually harm your financial situation. We are currently in a period when the rates for Know So Money options are at historic lows, and the volatility of Hope So Money is higher than ever. There is no overlapping acceptable rate, making both options less than ideal. *Because of this uncertain financial landscape, wise investment strategies are more important now than ever.*

This unique situation requires fresh ideas and investment tools that haven't been relied on in the past. Investing the way your parents did will not pay off. The majority of investment ideas used by financial professionals in the 1990s aren't applicable to today's markets. That kind of investing will likely get you in trouble and compromise your retirement. Today, you need a better PLAN.

A good plan is your first defense against risk. You might have a million dollars socked away in a savings account, but your neighbor, who has $300,000 in a diverse investment portfolio

THE ROAD LESS TRAVELED

that is tailored to their needs, may end up enjoying a better retirement lifestyle. Why? They had more than a good work ethic and a penchant for saving. They had a planful approach to retirement asset allocation.

CHAPTER 2 RECAP //

- A bad economy and a volatile market can make investors feel as if they are riding on a roller coaster. Without a plan and the guidance of a tax professional, investors acting alone can make changes to their portfolios that negatively affect their bottom line.

- When you take a loss on the stock market, you have to do more than just earn back your initial loss in order to get back to where you were before. The math of rebounds uses the percentage of the investment and not dollar amount to calculate what you need to earn in order to recapture your losses.

- Emotions inevitably enter the mix during stock market downturns. According to the DALBAR Quantitative Analysis of Investment Behavior report released in 2013, the average investor managing his or her money alone failed to keep up with inflation in nine out of the last 14 years.

- When looking at your different assets, it can be helpful to think of your money in terms of Hope So Money and Know So Money. Hope So money represents assets in the market that are exposed to risk. You hope that the money will be there for you in the future. Know So represents investments that are safe and guaranteed. The more Know So Money you have, the more peace of mind you will have during your retirement.

3

What Color is Your Money?

Over the course of your lifetime, it is likely that you have acquired a variety of assets. Assets can range from money that you have in a savings account or a 401(k), to a pension or an IRA. You have earned money and have made financial decisions based on the best information you had at the time. When viewed as a whole, however, you might not have an overall strategy for the management of your assets. As we have seen, it's more important than ever to know which of your assets are at risk. High market volatility and low treasury rates make for challenging financial topography. Navigating this financial landscape starts with planful asset management that takes into account your specific needs and options.

Even if you feel that you have plenty of money in your 401(k) or IRA, not knowing how much *risk* those investments are exposed to can cause you major financial suffering.

» *Abby was 66 and ready to retire. She had contributed faithfully to her company 401(k) plan and chose what she thought were very conservative stocks. Six years ago, Abby watched her friend, Carol, lose over $80,000 of her 401(k) investments after the market downturn of 2008. Abby didn't want that to happen to her, so she decided to go in and talk to a financial professional.*

"I don't want to take any risks," she said during the meeting. "So I'm only invested in conservative stocks." The financial professional took a look at Abby's 401(k) investments and discovered that it was invested 100 percent in stocks. "Do you realize," he told Abby, "That every dollar you have saved is currently sitting at risk?"

Abby had no idea.

A lot of people like Abby assume that investing in mutual funds or different classes of stocks or bonds mitigates risk and makes those investments less susceptible to market loss. This is a common illusion. Even the big companies such as Coca Cola lost as much as 38 percent during the market downturn. Most people don't know how much risk their retirement nest egg is exposed to. Visually organizing your assets is an important and powerful way to get a clear picture of what kind of money you have, where it is, and how you can best protect it so that it can provide you with an income in the future.

INTRODUCING THE "BASIC COLORS" OF CONSERVATIVE INVESTING

It can be helpful to assign colors to the different kinds of money and their level of risk. The colors will be familiar to you, because they correspond to the same colors as a traffic light: red, yellow and green. The same associations that you think of when operating a motor vehicle apply here to managing your retirement money.

Yellow: Yellow money is cash-type holdings and can be considered safe, Know So money. We all need some money in cash. These dollars are safe and liquid—meaning they can be spent—but they aren't making you any money. It might be tempting to keep all your money here in cash, but doing so presents its own risk because you lose purchasing power every day. Yellow Money doesn't earn significant returns. That's why this money is yellow—you have to be cautious. If you put too much of your money in Yellow Money investments you might outlive your assets. Yellow Money investments include the following:

- Checking
- Savings
- CD
- Money Market
- Fixed Annuity
- Fixed Life Insurance

Pros of Yellow Money: you can access Yellow Money any time. Yellow Money is safe and not at risk.

Cons of Yellow Money: In most cases, Yellow Money investments don't earn any significant rate of return and can't keep up with inflation.

Red: Red Money is growth money and is the opposite of Yellow Money. Red Money is sitting at risk, in the stock market, bond market (yes, you can lose money in bond funds), mutual funds—any market you can lose money in including real estate and commodities such as gold. Red Money is considered *Hope So Money* because there is no guarantee it will be there tomorrow. *Most* Red Money is also considered a mostly liquid asset, meaning it can be cashed in with relative ease. Just like with a traffic signal, you'll want to stop and think about the safety of these invest-

ments as your retirement years approach. Red Money investments include the following:
- Stocks
- Bonds
- Mutual Funds
- Exchange Trade Funds (ETF's)
- Options
- Precious Metals
- Variable Annuities
- Variable Universal Life Insurance

<u>Pros of Red Money</u>: You have the potential to grow your money and make unlimited profits. Red Money is also fairly liquid although there are some exceptions.

<u>Cons of Red Money</u>: You can lose unlimited amounts of money in Red Money investments. There are also fees associated with Red Money investments.

Green: Green Money exists between Yellow and Red money, and is what I call hybrid money. It has pieces of both Yellow and Red Money attributes. It has the safety of Yellow Money in that Green Money investments have a guaranteed principal. With a guaranteed principal, you typically can't lose any of the money you put into the investment. The earning potential of Green Money investments is also pretty good and in some cases, the rate of return can even be comparable to Red Money investments. Green money is *Know So Money* because there is no risk involved and you know it will be there when you need it. Green Money investments include the following:
- Fixed Index Annuity
- Fixed Index Life Insurance

<u>Pros of Green Money</u>: Green money is safe and protected. Typically these investments offer a competitive rate of return and have no fees.

<u>Cons of Green Money</u>: With Green Money investments you lose some liquidity. These investments are semi-liquid because you don't have access to the full cash value all the time.

Looking at your investments this way is what I think of as looking at your money from 30,000 feet in the air. It helps to get a bird's eye view and an overall picture of what you have and how much risk you are taking. It can also help to take the emotional element out of the investments. Sometimes people become unduly attached to a certain stock or mutual fund because "it's always done well for me in the past." As you near or enter retirement, the past no longer applies because you are going down the mountain now. You are no longer accumulating, which means you no longer have unlimited time to let your money grow.

There is nothing inherently good or bad about any investment you purchase or tool you use. There are only investments and tools that either help or hinder your goals. When you work with a financial professional, your job is to discover HOW much to put into each section—Red, Yellow or Green—depending on what goal you are trying to meet or fulfill.

THE RULES OF THE ROAD

The fact of the matter is that a lot of people don't know their level of exposure to risk. Visually organizing your assets is an important and powerful way to get a clear picture of what kind of money you have, where it is and how you can best use it in the future. This process is as simple as listing your assets and assigning them a color based on their status as Know So Money or Hope So Money. Work with your financial professional to create a comprehensive inventory of your assets to understand what you are working with before making any decisions. This may be the first time you have ever sat down and sorted out all of your assets, allowing you to see how much money you have at risk in the market. The following diagram can help shed some light on categorizing your individual assets by offering each money color with a set of rules or parameters it must meet in order to qualify for that color label.

The next step is to know the right amount and ratio of Green and Red Money for you at your stage of retirement planning. Investing heavily in Red Money and gambling all of your assets on the market is incredibly risky no matter where you fall on the retirement spectrum. Money in the market can't be depended on to generate income, and a plan that leans too heavily on Red Money can easily fail, especially when investment decisions are influenced by emotional reactions to market downturns and recoveries. Not only is this an unwise plan, it can be incredibly

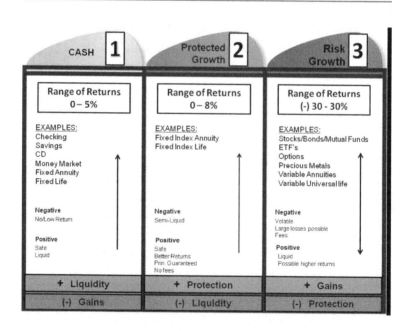

stressful to an investor who is in the need of stable income, but is gambling everything on stocks and mutual funds.

But a plan that uses too much Yellow Money avoids all volatility and can also fail. Why? Investing all of your money in Certificates of Deposit (CDs), savings accounts, money markets and other low return accounts may provide interest and income, but that likely won't be enough to keep pace with inflation and future retirement risks. If you focus exclusively on income from Yellow Money and avoid owning any stocks or mutual funds in your portfolio, you won't be able to leverage the potential for long-term growth your portfolio needs to stay healthy and productive.

This is where the Rule of 100 can help you determine how much of your money should be invested in the market to anticipate your future needs. Comparing the color of your investments will give you an idea of how near or far you are from adhering to the Rule of 100.

THE RULE OF 100: HOW MUCH CAN YOU COMFORTABLY RISK?

Determining the amount of risk that is right for you is dependent on a number of variables. You need to feel comfortable with where and how you are investing your money, and your financial professional is obligated to help you make decisions that put your money in places that fit your risk criteria.

Your retirement needs to first accommodate your day-to-day income needs. How much money do you need to maintain your lifestyle? When do you need it?

Managing your risk by having a balance of Hope So Money vs. Know So Money is a good start that will put you ahead of the curve. But how much Know So Money is enough to secure your income needs during retirement, and how much Hope So Money is enough to allow you to continue to benefit from an improving market?

In short, how do you begin to know how much risk you should be exposed to?

While there is no single approach to investment risk determination advice that is universally applicable to everyone, there are some helpful guidelines. One of the most useful is called *The Rule of 100.*

The average investor needs to accumulate assets to create a retirement plan that provides income during retirement and also allows for legacy planning. To accomplish this, they need to balance the amount of risk to which they are exposed. Risk is required because, while Yellow Money is safer, more reliable and more dependable, it doesn't grow very fast, if at all. Today's historically low interest rates barely break even with current inflation. Red Money, while less dependable, has more potential for growth. Red Money can eventually become Yellow or Green Money once you move it to an investment with lower risk. Everyone's risk diversification will be different depending on their goals, age and their existing assets.

So how do you decide how much risk *your* assets should be exposed to? Where do you begin? Luckily, there's a guideline you can use to start making decisions about risk management. It's called the Rule of 100.

CALCULATING YOUR RISK NUMBER

The Rule of 100 is a general rule that helps shape asset diversification* for the average investor. The rule states that the number 100

Asset Diversification disclosure – Diversification and asset allocation does not assure of guarantee better performance and cannot eliminate the risk of investment loss. Before investing, you should carefully read the applicable volatility disclosure for each of the underlying funds, which can be found in the current prospectus.

minus an investor's age equals the amount of assets they should have exposed to risk.

The Rule of 100: 100 - (your age) = the percentage of your assets that should be exposed to risk (Risk Side Money)

For example, if you are a 30-year-old investor, the Rule of 100 would indicate that you should be focusing on investing primarily in the market and taking on a substantial amount of risk in your portfolio. The Rule of 100 suggests that 70 percent of your investments should be exposed to risk.

100 - (30 years of age) = 70 percent

Now, not every 30-year-old should have exactly 70 percent of their assets in mutual funds and stocks. The Rule of 100 is based on your chronological age, not your "financial age," which could vary based on your investment experience, your aversion or acceptance of risk and other factors. While this rule isn't an ironclad solution to anyone's finances, it's a pretty good place to start. Once you've taken the time to look at your assets with a professional to determine your risk exposure, you can use the Rule of 100 to make changes that put you in a more stable investment position — one that reflects your comfort level.

Perhaps when you were age 30 and starting your career, like in the example above, it made sense to have 70 percent of your money in the market: you had time on your side. You had plenty of time to save more money, work more and recover from a downturn in the market. Retirement was ages away, and your earning power was increasing. And indeed, younger investors should take on more risk for exactly those reasons. The potential reward of long-term involvement in the market outweighs the risk of investing when you are young.

Risk tolerance generally reduces as you get older, however, if you are 40 years old and lose 30 percent of your portfolio in a market downturn this year, you have 20 or 30 years to recover it. If you are 68 years old, you have five to 10 years (or less) to make the same recovery. That new circumstance changes your whole retirement perspective. At age 68, it's likely that you simply aren't as interested in suffering through a tough stock market. There is less time to recover from downturns, and the stakes are higher. The money you have saved is money you will soon need to provide you with income, or is money that you already need to meet your income demands.

Much of the flexibility that comes with investing earlier in life is related to *compounding*. Compounded earnings can be incredibly powerful over time. The longer your money has time to compound, the greater your wealth will be. This is what most people talk about when they refer to putting their money to work. This is also why the Rule of 100 favors risk for the young. If you start investing when you are young, you can invest smaller amounts of money in a more aggressive fashion because you have the potential to make a profit in a rising market and you can harness the power of compounding earnings. When you are 40, 50 or 60 years old, that potential becomes less and less and you are forced to have more money at lower amounts of risk to realize the same returns. **It basically becomes more expensive to prudently invest the older you get.**

You risk not having a recovery period the older you get, so you should have less of your assets at risk in volatile investments. You should shift with the Rule of 100 to protect your assets and ensure that they will provide you with the income you need in retirement.

Let's look at another example that illustrates how the Rule of 100 becomes more critical as you age. An 80-year-old investor who is retired and is relying on retirement assets for income, for example, needs to depend on a solid amount of Yellow and Green Money. The Rule of 100 says an 80-year-old investor should have a maximum of 20 percent of his or her assets at risk. Depending on the investor's financial position, even less risk exposure may be required. You are the only person who can make this kind of determination, but the Rule of 100 can help. Everyone has their own level of comfort. Your Rule of 100 results will be based on your values and attitudes as well as your comfort with risk.

The Rule of 100 can apply to overarching financial management and to specific investment products that you own as well. Take the 401(k) for example. Many people have them, but not many people understand how their money is allocated within their 401(k). An employer may have someone who comes in once a year and explains the models and options that employees can choose from, but that's as much guidance as most 401(k) holders get. Many 401(k) options include target date funds that change their risk exposure over time, essentially following a form of the Rule of 100. Selecting one of these options can often be a good move for employees because they shift your risk as you age, securing more Green Money when you need it.

A financial professional can look at your assets with you and discuss alternatives to optimize your balance between Yellow, Green and Red Money.

OPTIMIZING RISK AND FINDING THE RIGHT BALANCE

Determining the amount of risk that is right for you depends on your specific situation and lifestyle considerations. It starts by examining your particular financial position.

The Rule of 100 is a useful way to begin to deliberate the right amount of risk for you. But remember, it's just a baseline. Use it as a starting point for figuring out where your money should be. If you're a 50-year-old investor, the Rule of 100 suggests that you have 50 percent Green Money and 50 percent Red Money. Most 50-year-olds are more risk tolerant. However, there are many reasons why someone might be more risk tolerant, not the least of which is feeling young! Experienced investors, people who feel they need to gamble for a higher return, or people who have met their retirement income goals and are looking for additional ways to accumulate wealth are all candidates for investment strategies that incorporate higher levels of risk. In the end, it comes down to your personal tolerance for risk. How much are you willing to lose?

Consulting with a financial professional is often the wisest approach to calculating your risk level. A professional can help determine your risk tolerance by getting to know you, asking you a set of questions and even giving you a survey to determine your comfort level with different types of risk. Here's a typical scenario a financial professional might pose to you:

"You have $100,000 saved that you would like to invest in the market. There is an investment product that could turn your $100,000 into $120,000. That same option, however, has the potential of losing you up to $30,000, leaving you with $70,000."

Is that a scenario that you are willing to enter into? Or are you more comfortable with this one:

"You could turn your $100,000 into $110,000, but have the potential of losing $15,000, leaving you with $85,000."

Your answer to these and others types of questions will help a financial professional determine what level of risk is right for you. They can then offer you investment strategies and management plans that reflect your financial age.

HELP STAYING ON THE ROAD

Once you've ironed out the crinkles in your roadmap and you're on your way, things happen. Whether the problem is car repairs, family issues or health related, you don't want to work with a financial professional who sells you something and then disappears.

> » Marie took a trip with her friend Julie from Savannah to Atlanta. Now this was just a four-plus-hour trip and so the two friends left after having a nice dinner together. Around eleven o'clock that night, Marie's husband gets a call. "I'm sorry to bother you," she says, "But it seems we took a wrong turn somewhere and the road we're on isn't in the GPS system. Can you please pull a map up on your computer and tell me where I am? Marie's husband Gary pulled up a map and after some discussion, the two of them figured out that Marie had taken a wrong turn about an hour and a half earlier. They were almost in Hilton Head. Gary gave Marie directions and got her started back on the road, going the right way this time. The mistake cost Marie about three hours in time and thirty dollars in gas, but it was a mistake that could have been a lot worse if she didn't have somebody to call.

When you go on a trip, you keep a look out for the road signs along the way, because these markers help to keep you going in the right direction. Your financial plan also has to be monitored. Things change in your life. From life changes such as the purchase of a new car to the gain of an inheritance, to big-picture changes in the economy, tax laws or stock market performance, things

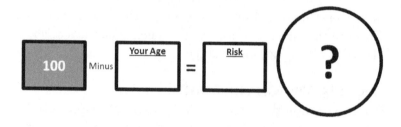

change. As you're driving along through retirement, there might be a sign that got knocked over, or the road is closed, washed out, or there's been a detour. Or maybe what's changed is your mind. You're bored with the desert and want to see some mountains. Whatever the reason for the change, you want to know that there is someone you can call to help get you turned around and headed in the right direction.

Financial professionals build careers around understanding the different variables affecting retirement financing. Working with a Registered Investment Advisor means working with a professional who is legally obligated to help you make financial decisions that are in your best interest and fall within your comfort zone. Taking steps toward creating a retirement plan is nothing to take lightly. By leveraging tax strategies, properly organizing your assets, and accumulating helpful financial products that help you meet your income and accumulation needs, you are more likely to stay on the road, meet your goals and get to where you are headed.

CHAPTER 3 RECAP //

- Multiple retirement accounts can create confusion about risk, distribution requirements and tax liabilities. Taking control of your assets begins with determining your exposure to risk.

- Assigning colors to money can help you more easily visualize the assets that make up your retirement savings. Green Money is safer and more reliable, Red Money represents assets that are exposed to risk, and Yellow Money is money kept in cash or savings accounts that you can readily access.

- Use the Rule of 100 as a general guiding principle when determining how much risk your retirement investments should be exposed to (100 - [your age] = [percentage of your investments that can comfortably be exposed to risk]).

- Your exposure to risk is ultimately determined by you.

- Working with a Registered Investment Advisor will help you compose a clear and concise inventory of your assets, and learn how much they are worth, what rules apply to them, and how they are structured for risk. A Registered Investment Advisor is legally obligated to help you make financial decisions that are in your best interest and fall within your comfort zone. They can also help you structure your investments so as to reflect your goals, needs and objectives.

4

Where is My Paycheck?

How much money do you need to be happy?

Jean was not happy. As a 66 year-old widow, she didn't have a stable income. She couldn't pick up the tab when going out to lunch with a friend, couldn't get repairs done or buy anything new. She was too afraid to spend money on travel and was driving around in what amounted to an old jalopy. This wasn't at all how she imagined her retirement would be. Her husband had made a good living while he was alive, and she knew he put aside money to take care of them. But every month she received the dividend checks from their various investments, and every month, the checks totaled up to a different amount. One month, she got $2,500, the next month, only $1,100. She was a grown woman trying to pay the bills and enjoy her retirement, yet she was living month-to-month, paycheck to paycheck. She hadn't seen her grandsons in over a year because she was too afraid to *spend the money. What if the next check came and it was only $200? Jean didn't know what she would do.*

Evaluating your income needs is the backbone of a good financial plan. If you want a paycheck during retirement, you have to figure out how to turn the assets you have into an income you can rely on, and you want to do it in a way that maximizes every dollar. Most people know how much income they need every month in retirement, because it's pretty close to what they need now. But they are usually surprised to find out how much money it takes to create that income.

Advice about how to invest money has been around forever. Good advice, however, changes with the times. Back in the old days, people were advised to keep their money invested in the stock market and take out five percent to live on. This was the advice Jean in our story example above was following. Relying on old advice won't get you very far today. Keeping your assets in Red Money accounts exposes them to a new and volatile market. You can't take out that five percent without exposing yourself to the risk of losing as much as 50 percent of your principal. With this kind of volatility, you would need to take out closer to two to three percent in order to maintain your principal, and living off two percent means the nest egg you start with has to be pretty big.

It is possible to create a stable source of income using Green Money sources. It's possible to create your own personal pension plan using the investments you do have with the help of a financial professional. This is the biggest thing that working with a financial professional can do for you during your retirement years: they can deliver peace of mind so you can go and enjoy your life. Like Jean in our story example, you might be afraid to spend your money, afraid to travel and afraid to enjoy your retirement life. Peace of mind comes from knowing your income needs are met.

HOW MUCH AND WHEN

Because circumstances often arise, the best income plans allow for flexibility and change. Using the goals you identified in chapter one, creating an income plan begins with an evaluation of your daily needs. Finding the most efficient and beneficial way to address them will have impacts on your lifestyle, your asset accumulation and your legacy planning after you retire. When you have identified your goals and income needs, you will know how much to structure for income and how much to be set aside for accumulation.

Every financial strategy for retirement needs first to accommodate the day-to-day need to pay the bills. The moment your working income ceases and you start living off the money you've set aside for retirement is referred to as the retirement cliff. When you begin drawing income from your retirement assets, you have entered the distribution phase of your financial plan. The distribution phase of your retirement plan is when you reach the point of relying on your assets for income. This is where your Green Money comes into play: the safer, more reliable assets that you have accumulated that are designed to provide you with a steady income. On day one of your retirement, you will need a steady and reliable supply of income from your Green Money.

How Much Money Do You Need? While this amount will be different for everyone, the general rule of thumb is that a retiree will require 70 to 80 percent of their pre-retirement income to maintain their lifestyle. Once you know what that number is, the key becomes matching your income need with the correct investment strategies, options and tools to satisfy that need.

When Do You Need Your Money? If you need income to last 10 years, use a tool that creates just that. If you need a lifetime of income, seek a tool that will do that and won't run out.

51

TURNING ON THE STREAMS

The most common sources of income during retirement are pensions, Social Security benefits, and accumulated money set up in 401(k)s, traditional and ROTH IRAs. Identify the source and the amount of the income, as well as its frequency.

Next, determine when those streams need to be turned on, and how long they need to run. Ask yourself, when do you need the money? And how long do you need the money? As mentioned earlier, the best plans are those that aren't cast in stone. They allow for some flexibility. If there is an inheritance that may come into effect somewhere down the road, or if the death of a spouse occurs, your income needs will change. Slowing down or switching off those income streams should be options built into your plan so it can be adjusted to life's changing needs.

Green Money becomes much more important as you age. While you want to reduce the amount of Red Money you have and transition it to Green Money, you don't necessarily need all of it to generate income for you right away. Taking a closer look at Green Money, you will see there are actually different types.

TYPES OF GREEN MONEY:
NEED NOW AND NEED LATER

Money that you need to depend on for income is Green Money. Once you have filled the income gap at the beginning of your retirement, you may have money left over.

There are two types of Green Money: money used for income and money used for accumulation to meet your income needs in five, 10 or 20 years. Money needed for income is Need Now Money. It is money you need to meet your basic needs, to pay your bills, your mortgage if you have one and the costs associated with maintaining your lifestyle. Money used for accumulation is Need Later Money. It's money that you don't need now for income, but will need to rely on down the road. It's still Green

Money because you will rely on it later for income and will need to count on it being there. Need Later Money represents income your assets will need to generate for future use. When planning your retirement, it is vital to decide how much of your assets to structure for income and how much to set aside to accumulate to create Need Later Money.

You must figure out if your income and accumulation needs are met. Your Need Now and Need Later Money are top priorities. Need Now Money, in particular, will dictate what your options for future needs are. Need Later Money can often be subject to more risk, because these investments are designed to be left alone until needed 10 or 20 years down the road. This is another opportunity to evaluate your investments in terms of risk and Red Money investments.

THE NUMBERS DON'T LIE

When the rubber meets the road, the numbers dictate your options. Your risk tolerance is an important indicator of what kinds of investments you should consider, but if the returns from those investments don't meet your retirement goals, your income needs will likely not be met. For example, if the level of risk you are comfortable with manages your investments at a 4 percent return and you need to realize an 8 percent return, your income needs aren't going to be met when you need to rely on your investments for retirement income. A professional may encourage you to be more aggressive with your investment strategy by taking on more risk in order to give you the potential of earning a greater return. If taking more risk isn't an option that you are comfortable with, then the discussion will turn to how you can earn more money or spend less in order to align your needs with your resources more closely.

How are you going to structure your income flow during retirement? The answer to this question dictates how you determine your risk tolerance. If the numbers say that you need to be more aggressive with your investing, or that you need to modify your lifestyle, it becomes a choice you need to make.

Take a moment to think about your retirement goals:
- What is your lifestyle today?
- Would you like to maintain it into retirement?
- Are you meeting your needs?
- Are you happy with your lifestyle?
- What do you really *need* to live on when you retire?

Some people will have the luxury of maintaining or improving their lifestyle, while others may have to make decisions about what they need versus what they want during their retirement.

As we determined earlier, the most important thing you need to do as you create an income plan is to take care to avoid too much exposure to risk. You can start by meeting with an Investment Advisor to organize your assets. Get your Green Money and Red Money in order and balanced to meet your needs. If the market goes down 18 percent this afternoon, you don't want that to come out of what you're relying on for next year's income. Hot on the heels of securing your Green Money, it's time to structure those Green Money assets so they can generate income for you. Ultimately, you have to take care of your monthly income needs to pay the bills.

The Big Kahuna of Green Money and income? Your Social Security benefit.

CHAPTER 4 RECAP //

- Outliving their money is what retirees fear the most. Build your retirement income from the sound foundation of Green Money, or Know So Money. The foundation of a retirement strategy depends on knowing how much money you need and when you need it.

- Identify how much of your income you need now, and how much you need later. Once you have your current Need Now income needs supplied, it's crucial to the longevity of your income to plan for Need Later Money. This offers another opportunity to look at Red Money investments for growth.

- Working with a Registered Investment Advisor will help you compose a clear and concise inventory of your assets, and learn how much they are worth, what rules apply to them, and how they are structured for risk.

5

Don't Leave Money On The Table
Maximizing Social Security

Does it matter when I start taking my Social Security benefit?

Mary had worked full-time nearly her entire adult life and was looking forward to enjoying retirement with her husband, kids and grandkids. When she turned 62, she decided to take advantage of her Social Security benefits as soon as they became available.

A couple of years later, she was organizing some of the paperwork in her home office. She came across an old Social Security statement, and remembered the feeling of filing and beginning a new phase in her life.

However, as she looked over the statement, she realized in retrospect that she might have been better off waiting to file for benefits. She had saved enough to wait for benefits, and if she had, her monthly benefit could have been quite a bit more.

When she was in the process of retiring, there were so many other decisions to make. It seemed very straightforward to file right away. She made a note to call the Social Security Administration to see if it was possible to change her monthly benefit to the larger amount.

One kind of Green Money that most Americans can rely on for income when they retire is Social Security. If you're like most Americans, Social Security is or will be an important part of your retirement income and one that you should know how to properly manage. As a first step in creating your income plan, a financial professional will take a look at your Social Security benefit options. Social Security is the foundation of income planning for anyone who is about to retire and is a reliable source of Green Money in your overall income plan.

Here are some facts that illustrate how Americans currently use Social Security:

- Nearly 90 percent of Americans age 65 and older receive Social Security benefits.*
- Social Security provides about 39 percent of the income of the elderly.*
- Claiming Social Security benefits at the wrong time can reduce your monthly benefit by up to 65 percent.**
- In 2013, 36 percent of men and 40 percent of women claimed Social Security benefits at age 62.***
- In 2013, more than a third of workers claimed Social Security benefits as soon they became eligible.***

---

* *https://www.ssa.gov/pressoffice/basicfact.html*

** *https://www.ssa.gov/planners/retire/retirechart.html*

*** *Trends in Social Security Claiming, Alicia H Munnell and Anqi Chen, Center for Retirement Research, May 2015. http://crr.bc.edu/wp-content/uploads/2015/05/IB_15-8.pdf*

- In 2015, the average monthly Social Security benefit was $1,328. The maximum benefit for 2015 was $2,663. *The $1,335 monthly benefit reduction between the average and the maximum is applied for life.* *

There are many aspects of Social Security that are well known and others that aren't. When it comes time for you to cash in on your Social Security benefit, you will have many options and choices. Social Security is a massive government program that manages retirement benefits for millions of people. Experts spend their entire careers understanding and analyzing it. Luckily, you don't have to understand all of the intricacies of Social Security to maximize its advantages. You simply need to know the best way to manage your Social Security benefit. You need to know exactly what to do to get the most from your Social Security benefit and when to do it. Taking the time to create a roadmap for your Social Security strategy will help ensure that you are able to exact your maximum benefit and efficiently coordinate it with the rest of your retirement plan.

There are many aspects of Social Security that you have no control over. You don't control how much you put into it, and you don't control what it's invested in or how the government manages it. However, you do control when and how you file for benefits. The real question about Social Security that you need to answer is, "When should I start taking Social Security?" While this is the all-important question, there are a couple of key pieces of information you need to track down first.

Before we get into a few calculations and strategies that can make all the difference, let's start by covering the basic information about Social Security which should give you an idea of where you stand. Just as the foundation of a house creates the stable platform for the rest of the framework to rest upon, your Social

---

* *https://www.ssa.gov/news/press/factsheets/colafacts2015.html*

Security benefit is an important part of your overall retirement plan. The purpose of the information that follows is not to give an exhaustive explanation of how Social Security works, but to give you some tools and questions to start understanding how Social Security affects your retirement and how you can prepare for it.

Let's start with eligibility.

Eligibility. Understanding how and when you are eligible for Social Security benefits will help clarify what to expect when the time comes to claim them.

To receive retirement benefits from Social Security, you must earn eligibility. In almost all cases, Americans born after 1929 must earn 40 quarters of credit to be eligible to draw their Social Security retirement benefit. In 2015, a Social Security credit represents $1,220 earned in a calendar quarter. The number changes as it is indexed each year, but not drastically. In 2014, a credit represented $1,200. Four quarters of credit is the maximum number that can be earned each year. In 2015, an American would have had to earn at least $4,880 to accumulate four credits. In order to qualify for retirement benefits, you must have earned a minimum number of credits. Additionally, if you are at least 62 years old and have been married to a recipient of Social Security benefits for at least 12 months, you can choose to receive Spousal Benefits. Although 40 is the minimum number of credits required to begin drawing benefits, it is important to know that once you claim your Social Security benefit, there is no going back. Although there may be cost of living adjustments made, you are locked into that base benefit amount forever.

Primary Insurance Amount. You can think of your Primary Insurance Amount (PIA) like a ripening fruit. It represents the amount of your Social Security benefit at your Full Retirement Age (FRA). Your benefit becomes fully ripe at your FRA, and will neither reduce nor increase due to early or delayed retirement options. If you opt to take benefits before your FRA, however, your monthly benefit will be less than your PIA. You will essentially be picking an unripened fruit. On the one hand, waiting until after your FRA to access your benefits will increase your benefit beyond your PIA. On the other hand, you don't want the fruit to overripen, because every month you wait is one less check you get from the government.

Full Retirement Age. Your FRA is an important figure for anyone who is planning to rely on Social Security benefits in their retirement. Depending on when you were born, there is a specific age at which you will attain FRA. Your FRA is dictated by your year of birth and is the age at which you can begin your full monthly benefit. Your FRA is important because it is half of the equation used to calculate your Social Security benefit. The other half of the equation is based on when you start taking benefits.

When Social Security was initially set up, the FRA was age 65, and it still is for people born before 1938. But as time has passed, the age for receiving full retirement benefits has increased. If you were born between 1938 and 1960, your full retirement age is somewhere on a sliding scale between 65 and 67. Anyone born in 1960 or later will now have to wait until age 67 for full benefits. Increasing the FRA has helped the government reduce the cost of the Social Security program, which paid out almost $870 billion to beneficiaries in 2015!*

While you can begin collecting benefits as early as age 62, the amount you receive as a monthly benefit will be less than it would be if you wait until you reached your FRA or surpass your FRA. It is important to note that if you file for your Social Security benefit before your FRA, *the reduction to your monthly benefit will remain in place for the rest of your life.* You can also delay

---

* *https://www.ssa.gov/news/press/basicfact.html*

receiving benefits up to age 70, in which case your benefits will be higher than your PIA for the rest of your life.

- At FRA, 100 percent of PIA is available as a monthly benefit.
- At age 62, your Social Security retirement benefits are available. For each month you take benefits prior to your FRA, however, the monthly amount of your benefit is reduced. **This reduction stays in place for the rest of your life.**
- At age 70, your monthly benefit reaches its maximum. After you turn age 70, your monthly benefit will no longer increase.

Year of Birth	Full Retirement Age
1943-1954	66
1955	66 and 2 months
1956	66 and 4 months
1957	66 and 6 months
1958	66 and 8 months
1959	66 and 10 months
1960 or later	age 67*

ROLLING UP YOUR SOCIAL SECURITY

Your Social Security income "rolls up" the longer you wait to claim it. Your monthly benefit will continue to increase until you turn 70 years old. Even though Social Security is the foundation of most people's retirement, many Americans feel that they don't have control over how or when they receive their benefits. The truth is that every dollar you increase your Social Security income by means less money you will have to spend from your nest egg to meet your retirement income needs, but many retirees do not

---

* *http://www.ssa.gov/OACT/progdata/nra.html*

take advantage of this fact. For many people, creating their Social Security strategy is the most important decision they can make to positively impact their retirement. *The difference between the best and worst Social Security decision can be tens of thousands of dollars over a lifetime of benefits.*

Deciding NOW or LATER: Following the above logic, it makes sense to wait as long as you can to begin receiving your Social Security benefit. However, the answer isn't always that simple. Not everyone has the option of waiting. Many people need to rely on Social Security on day one of their retirement. Some might need the income. Others might be in poor health and don't feel they will live long enough to make FRA worthwhile for themselves or their families. It is also possible, however, that the majority of folks taking an early benefit at age 62 are simply under-informed about Social Security. Perhaps they make this major decision based on rumors and emotion.

File Immediately if You:
- Find your job is unbearable.
- Are willing to sacrifice retirement income.
- Are not healthy and need a reliable source of income.

Consider Delaying Your Benefit if You:
- Want to maximize your retirement income.
- Want to increase retirement benefits for your spouse.
- Are still working and like it.
- Are healthy and willing / able to wait to file.

So if you decide to wait, how long should you wait? Lots of people can put it off for a few years, but not everyone can wait until they are 70 years old. Your individual circumstances may be able to help you determine when you should begin taking Social Security.

THE ROAD LESS TRAVELED

If you do the math, you will quickly see that between ages 62 and 70, there are 96 months in which you can file for your Social Security benefit. If you take into account those 96 months and the 96 months your spouse could also file for Social Security, the number of different strategies for structuring your benefit, you can easily end up with more than 20,000 different scenarios. It's safe to say this isn't the kind of math that most people can easily handle. Each month would result in a different benefit amount. The longer you wait, the higher your monthly benefit amount becomes. Each month you wait, however, is one less month that you receive a Social Security check.

The goal is to maximize your lifetime benefits. That may not always mean waiting until you can get the largest monthly payment. Taking the bigger picture into account, you want to find out how to get the most money out of Social Security over the number of years that you draw from it. Don't underestimate the power of optimizing your benefit: the difference between the BEST and WORST Social Security election can easily be worth thousands of dollars in lifetime benefits. *The difference can be very substantial!*

If you know that every month you wait, your Social Security benefit goes up a little bit, and you also know that every month you wait, you receive one less benefit check, how do you determine where the sweet spot is that maximizes your benefits over your lifetime? Financial professionals have access to software that will calculate the best year and month for you to file for benefits based on your default life expectancy. You can further customize that information by estimating your life expectancy based on your health, habits and family history. If you can then create an income plan (we'll get into this later in the chapter) that helps you wait until the target date for you to file for Social Security, you can optimize your retirement income strategy to get the most out of your Social Security benefit. How can you calculate your life expectancy? Well, you don't know exactly how long you'll live, but you have a better idea than the government does. They rely on averages to make their calculations. You have much more personal information about your health, lifestyle and family history than they do. You can use that knowledge to game the system and beat all the other people who are making uninformed decisions by filing early for Social Security.

While you can and should educate yourself about how Social Security works, the reality is you don't need to know a lot of general information about Social Security in order to make choices about your retirement. What you do need to know is exactly what to do to maximize your benefit. Because knowing what you need to do has huge impacts on your retirement! For most Americans, Social Security is the foundation of income planning for retirement. Social Security benefits represent about 39 percent of the income of the elderly.* For many people, it can represent the largest portion of their retirement income. Not treating your Social Security benefit as an asset and investment tool can lead to sub-optimization of your largest source of retirement income.

Let's take a look at an example that shows the impact of working with a financial professional to optimize Social Security benefits:

> » *George and Mary Bailey are a typical American couple who have worked their whole lives and saved when they could. George is 60 years old, and Mary is 56 years old. They sat down with a financial professional who logged onto the Social Security website to look up their PIAs. George's PIA is $1,900 and Mary's is $900.*
>
> *If the Baileys cash in at age 62 and begin taking retirement benefits from Social Security, they will receive an estimated $568,600 in lifetime benefits. That may seem like a lot, but if you divide that amount over 20 years, it averages*

---

* https://www.socialsecurity.gov/pressoffice/basicfact.html

out to around $28,400 per year. The Baileys are accustomed to a more significant annual income than that. To make up the difference, they will have to rely on alternative retirement income options. They will basically have to depend on a bigger nest egg to provide them with the income they need.

If they wait until their FRA, they will increase their lifetime benefits to an estimated $609,000. This option allows them to achieve their Primary Insurance Amount, which will provide them a $34,200 annual income.

After learning the Baileys' needs and using software to calculate the most optimal time to begin drawing benefits, the Baileys' financial professional determined that the best option for them drastically increases their potential lifetime benefits to $649,000!

By using strategies that their financial professional recommended, they increased their potential lifetime benefits by as much as $80,000. There's no telling how much you could miss out on from your Social Security if you don't take time to create a strategy that calculates your maximum benefit. For the Baileys, the value of maximizing their benefits was the difference between night and day. While this may seem like a special case, it isn't uncommon to find benefit increases of this magnitude. You'll never know unless you take a look at your own options.

Despite the importance of knowing when and how to take your Social Security benefit, many of today's retirees and pre-retirees may know little about the mechanics of Social Security and how they can maximize their benefit.

So, to whom should you turn for advice when making this complex decision? Before you pick up the phone and call Uncle Sam, you should know that the Social Security Administration (SSA) representatives are actually prohibited from giving you election advice! Plus, SSA representatives in general are trained to focus on monthly benefit amounts, not the lifetime income for a family.

MAXIMIZING YOUR LIFETIME BENEFIT

As discussed earlier, calculating how to maximize lifetime benefits is more important than waiting until age 70 for your maximum monthly benefit amount. It's about getting the most income during your lifetime. Professional benefit maximization software can target the year and month that it is most beneficial for you to file based on your life expectancy.

The three most common ages that people associate with retirement benefits are 62 (Earliest Eligible Age), 66 (Full Retirement Age), and 70 (age at which monthly maximum benefit is reached). In almost all circumstances, however, none of those three most common ages will give you the maximum lifetime benefit.

Remember, every month you wait to file, the amount of your benefit check goes up, but you also get one less check. You don't know how exactly how long you're going to live, but you have a better idea of your life expectancy than the actuaries at the Social Security Administration who can only work with averages. They can't make calculations based on your specific situation. A professional can run the numbers for you and get the target date that maximizes your potential lifetime benefits. You can't get this information from the SSA, but you can get it from a financial professional.

Types of Social Security Benefits:

- *Retired Worker Benefit.* This is the benefit with which most people are familiar. The Retired Worker Benefit is what most people are talking about when they refer to Social Security. It is your benefit based on your earnings and the

67

amount that you have paid into the system over the span of your career.

- *Spousal Benefit.* This is available to the spouse of someone who is eligible for Retired Worker Benefits.
- *Survivorship Benefit.* When one spouse passes away, the survivor is able to receive the larger of the two benefit amounts.
- *Restricted Application.* A higher-earning spouse may be able to start collecting a spousal benefit on the lower-earning spouse's benefit while allowing his or her benefit to continue to grow. Due to the Bipartisan Budget Act of 2015, this option is only available to individuals who turn age 62 before January 1, 2016.

In November of 2015, the Bipartisan Budget Act of 2015 was passed, which will have a dramatic impact on the way many Americans plan for Social Security. As the largest change to Social Security since 2000, the Bipartisan Budget Act of 2015 eliminated an estimated $9.5 billion* of benefits to retirees and may limit some of the flexibility you previously had to structure your benefits.

In 2000, Congress passed the Senior Citizens Freedom to Work Act. The bill allowed retirees to suspend receiving benefits so they wouldn't be subject to additional taxation if they chose to return to work after they filed for Social Security. However, by doing so, the bill also unintentionally created several loopholes in claiming strategies: most notably, the Restricted Application for spousal benefits and "file and suspend" filing strategy. For most Americans, the Bipartisan Budget Act of 2015 closed the loopholes by eliminating "file and suspend" and the Restricted Application.

---

* *https://www.nasdaq.com/article/congress-planning-to-close-social-security-loopholes-cm536252*

The new rules mandate that:

- If a primary worker is not currently receiving benefits, then their dependents (child, spouse) can no longer collect benefits based on the primary worker's earning record.
- If you file for benefits, then you are filing for all benefits to which you are entitled – not just the benefit type you choose.

It's important to remember that in spite of these immense changes, one thing stayed the same – filing for Social Security is one of the most important financial decisions you will make in your lifetime, and a financial professional can help ensure you make the right one.

THE DIVORCE FACTOR

How does a divorced spouse qualify for benefits? If you have gone through a divorce, it might affect the retirement benefit to which you are entitled.

In general, a person can receive benefits as a divorced spouse on a former spouse's Social Security record so long as the following conditions are met:

- the marriage lasted at least 10 years; and
- the person filing for divorced benefits is at least age 62, unmarried, and not entitled to a higher Social Security benefit on his or her own record.*

With all of the different options, strategies and benefits to choose from, you can see why filing for Social Security is more complicated than just mailing in the paperwork. Gathering the data and making yourself aware of all your different options isn't enough to know exactly what to do, however. On the one hand, you can knock yourself out trying to figure out which options are best

---

* *https://www.ssa.gov/retire2/yourdivspouse.html*

for you and wondering if you made the best decision. On the other hand, you can work with a financial professional who uses customized software that takes all the variables of your specific situation into account and calculates your best option. You have tens of thousands of different options for filing for your Social Security benefit. If your spouse is a different age than you are, it nearly doubles the amount of options you have. This is far more complicated arithmetic than most people can do on their own. If you want a truly accurate understanding of when and how to file, you need someone who will ask you the right questions about your situation, someone who has access to specialized software that can crunch the numbers. The reality is that you need to work with a professional that can provide you with the sophisticated analysis of your situation that will help you make a truly informed decision.

Important Questions about Your Social Security Benefit:
- How can I maximize my lifetime benefit? By knowing when and how to file for Social Security. This usually means waiting until you have at least reached your Full Retirement Age. A professional has the experience and the tools to help determine when and how you can maximize your lifetime benefits.
- Who will provide reliable advice for making these decisions? Only a professional has the tools and experience to provide you reliable advice.
- Will the Social Security Administration provide me with the advice? The Social Security Administration cannot provide you with advice or strategies for claiming your benefit. They can give you information about your monthly benefit, but that's it. They also don't have the tools to tell you what your specific best option is. They can accurately answer how the system works, but they can't

advise you on what decision to make as to how and when to file for benefits.

The Maximization Report that your financial professional will generate represents an invaluable resource for understanding how and when to file for your Social Security benefit. When you get your customized Social Security Maximization Report, you will not only know all the options available to you – but you will understand the financial implications of each choice. In addition to the analysis, you will also get a report that shows exactly at what age – including which month and year – you should trigger benefits and how you should apply. It also includes a variety of other time-specific recommendations, such as when to apply for Medicare or take Required Minimum Distributions from your qualified plans. A report means there is no need to wonder, or to try to figure out when to take action – the Social Security Maximization Report lays it all out for you in plain English.

CHAPTER 5 RECAP //

- You cannot get advice about how to maximize your lifetime benefit from a Social Security representative. They are prohibited from giving advice about when to elect your benefit options.

- To get the most out of your Social Security benefit, you need to file at the right time. Every dollar your Social Security income increases is less money you'll have to spend from your retirement savings to supplement your income.

- An Investment Advisor can help you determine when you should file for Social Security to get your Maximum Lifetime Benefit.

- Deciding when to take your Social Security benefit is one of the most important decisions you make as a retiree. After the first year of taking the benefit, that amount is locked in for the duration of your lifetime.

- Social Security is a massive, government-funded program and there are many things about this program that you cannot control. You can, however, control when and how you file for benefits.

6

What If I Need More Money?
Tools To Help Fill The Income Gap

Use the right tool for the job.

Frederick and his wife just bought their first house. One fine summer afternoon in a Georgia July, Frederick's wife decided he should plant an azalea bush in the back yard. Now, July in Georgia means 95 degrees Fahrenheit and 90 percent humidity. Georgia also has red clay, roots and stones. But Frederick loved his sweetheart and so he got a shovel and started digging. After about two hours, he had about half a hole, or half of what he needed, and he was panting. His hands were covered in blisters and there wasn't a dry place anywhere on his body. He wasn't at all happy, but what's a husband to do?

Frederick was leaning on his shovel, taking a rest, when his neighbor, Phillip ambled by. Phillip peered over the fence, chuckled, and asked, "Whatcha doing?" Frederick wasn't a big fan of Phillip to begin with, but he entertained a conversation for the sake of manners. He explained how he was digging a hole. Phillip shook his head, chuckled again and left.

Now Frederick was more than a little peeved. He was hot, uncomfortable, in pain, and Phillip had laughed at him. Not only that, but he didn't even offer to help. Frederick started back at his digging.

A few minutes later Phillip appeared by his side with a different shovel. "Use this," he said, "It will be much easier."

"But I already have a shovel," Frederick explained.

"Yes," said Phillip, "You have a shovel, but not the right shovel for the job. To dig a hole, you need a spade. What you have there is for scooping."

Frederick took the new shovel and finished digging his hole within 20 minutes.

The moment that you stop working and start living off the money that you've set aside for retirement can be referred to as the Retirement Cliff. You've worked and earned money your whole life, but the day that you retire, that income comes to an end. That's the day that you have to have other assets that fill the gap. Social Security will fill in some, but you need to come up with something else. After you have calculated your Social Security benefit and have selected the year and month that will maximize your lifetime benefits, it's time to look at your other retirement assets, incomes and options that will reduce or eliminate the drop-off of the Retirement Cliff. You may have a pension, an IRA or Roth IRA, dividends from stock holdings, money from the sale of real estate, rental property, or other sources of income. What other sources of reliable income do you have?

Like Frederick in our story example above, you want the right investment tool for the job. There was nothing wrong with Frederick's shovel—it fit his hands and was of high quality. ***But he was using it for the wrong job***. It's easy to become attached to certain tools in the shed because we've always had them. It's also just as easy to become prejudiced against certain investment tools because when we tried them in the past, they were lousy. Remember, the investment itself isn't necessarily good or bad. Its value lies in whether or not it's the right tool for the job.

In order to grow money for Need Later needs, bank CDs and money market accounts are not generating enough interest to keep up with the combined factors of inflation and taxes. On the other hand, stocks, bonds and mutual funds have risks attached to them. Is there an investment tool out there that is the right tool for the job?

Today's annuities have been designed to solve problems specific to today's retirees. They work very much like Social Security in that they give you that reliable pension check every month, but that's not all they can do. A long term care rider can also be added to your annuity at the time of its purchase. Adding a long term care rider can provide you or your spouse with an income doubler should one of you need to fund the cost of long term care during your lifetime. A linked benefit is another word for a long term care benefit, also known as Living Benefits. Living Benefits provide you with money *while you are still alive* to cover the expense of home health care and long term care. Annuities are a life insurance product and there are many different kinds of annuities you can purchase to fill your income gap and address other income concerns.

Ask yourself the following questions:
- How concerned are you about finding a secure financial vehicle to protect your savings?
- How concerned are you that there may be a better way to structure your savings?

If you are concerned about the best way to fill your income gap, an income annuity investment tool is likely a good option for you. Income annuities have many similar qualities to Social Security that give them the same look and feel as that reliable benefit check you get every month. Most importantly, an income annuity can be an efficient and profitable way to solve your income gap.

DIFFERENT TYPES OF ANNUITIES AND WHAT THEY CAN DO

The word annuity as defined by the fourth edition of the American Heritage Dictionary as "the annual payment of an allowance or income." Annuities are popular and reliable investment tools that allow you to secure income during retirement. In its simplest form, annuities offer a way to invest money that allows you to structure it for income. There are many different kinds of annuities and finding the right one for you will take a conversation with your financial professional. Be sure you fully understand the features, benefits and costs of any annuity you are considering before investing money.

Fixed Indexed Annuities (FIAs) with no bells or whistles (and no income riders) are designed to be a Green Money way to grow your Need Later Money. They are tied to an index, such as the S&P 500 or commodities in the market place, and as a result are able to earn higher gains than Yellow Money options such as bank CD's. They are sold by an insurance company, tied to the index of your choice, and you can't lose your principal due to market fluctuations.

Variable annuities can lose money due to market fluctuations. As their name suggests, they vary with the stock market and the value of the principal is not guaranteed. If you purchase an income rider on a variable annuity, the Income Account Value will stay the same, but the value of your *actual* contract may fall. If you surrender the annuity, the insurance company will pay you the market value of the asset, regardless of whether it matches, exceeds or falls short of the value at which you bought the contract. If its value has dropped significantly, you may be better off taking the income rider as an income-for-life stream without surrendering your contract.

Here is how fixed indexed annuities can work:
When you put your money into an annuity, you are essentially buying an investment product from an insurance company. It is a contract between you and the insurance company that provides the investment tool. Let's say you have saved $100,000 and need it to generate income to meet your needs above and beyond your Social Security and pension checks. You give the $100,000 to an insurance company, who in turn invests it to generate growth.

They usually select investments that have modest returns over long term horizons. In other words, they generally put it somewhere stable and predictable. Most commonly, they will invest it in a combination of bonds and treasuries that are safer and dependable ways to grow money. They use the money from the insurance products they sell to invest, use a portion of the returns to generate profits for themselves, and return a portion to clients in the form of payouts, claims, and structured income options.

One of the most attractive qualities of these types of annuities is something called annual reset. Annual reset is sometimes also referred to as a "ratcheting." It works very much like a tire jack that holds up your car. The ratchet allows you to push that heavy car up one notch at a time, but it can't fall back down (which is a good thing, because usually somebody is underneath it, doing repair.) So, too, an annuity with an annual reset won't drop with the market and lose principal.

It works like this: If the market goes down, you don't suffer a loss. Instead, the insurance company absorbs it. But if the market goes up, you share with the insurance company some of the profit made on the gain. The amount of gain you get is called your annuity participation rate. Typically the insurer will cap the amount of gain you can realize at somewhere between 3 and 7 percent. If the market goes up 10 percent, you would realize a portion of that gain (whatever percentage you are capped at). This means you to never lose money on your investment, while always gaining a portion of the upswings. The measurement period of your annuity can be calculated monthly, weekly and even daily, but most annuities are measured annually. The level of the index when you buy and the index level one year later will determine the amount of loss or gain. You and the insurance company are betting that the market will generally go up over time.

HOW INCOME RIDERS WORK

When you use that $100,000 to buy a contract with an insurance company in the form of a fixed indexed annuity, you are pegging your money on an index. It could be the S&P 500, the Dow Jones Industrial Average or any number of indexes. To generate income from the annuity, you select something called an income rider. An income rider is a subset of an indexed annuity. Essentially, it is the amount of money from which the insurance company will pay you an income while you have your money in their annuity. Your income rider is a larger number than what your investment is actually worth, and if you select the income rider, it will increase in value over time, providing you with more income. As the insurance company holds your money and invests it, they generate a return on it that they use to pay you a regular monthly income based on a higher number. The insurance company has to outperform the amount that they pay you in order to make a profit.

Remember, insurance companies make long-term investments that provide them with predictable flows of money. They like to stabilize the amount of money that goes in and out of their doors instead of paying and receiving large unpredictable chunks at once. When you opt for an income rider, an insurance company can reliably predict how much money they will pay out to you over a set period of time. It's predictable, and they like that. They can base their business on those predictable numbers.

In order to encourage investors to leave their money in their annuity contracts, insurance companies create surrender periods that protect their investments. If you remove your money from the annuity contract during the surrender period, you will pay a penalty and will not be able to receive your entire investment amount back. A typical surrender period is 10 years. If after three years you decide that you want your $100,000 back, the insurance company has that money tied up in bonds and other investments with the understanding that they will have it for another seven years. Because they will take a hit on removing the money from

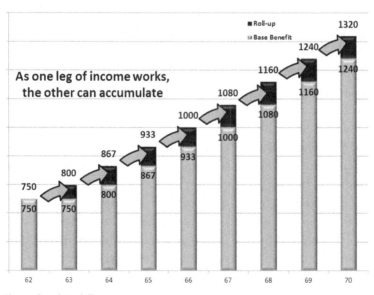

This is a hypothetical illustration

their investments prematurely, you will have to pay a surrender charge that makes up for their loss. During the surrender period, an annuity is not a demand deposit account like a savings or checking account. The higher returns that you are guaranteed from an annuity are dependent on the timeframe you selected. The longer an insurance company can hold your money, the easier it is for them to guarantee a predictable return on it.

If you leave your money in the annuity contract, you get a reliable monthly income no matter what happens in the market. Once the surrender period has expired, you can remove your money whenever you want. Your money becomes liquid again because the insurance company used it in an investment that fit the timeline of your surrender period. For many people, this is an attractive trade off that can provide a creative solution for filling their income gap.

OTHER BENEFITS AND OPTIONS

When is an annuity with an income rider right for you? A good financial professional can help you make that determination by taking the time to listen closely to your situation and understanding what your needs are as you enter retirement. Every salesperson has a bag full of brochures and PowerPoint presentations, but they need to know exactly what the financial concerns of their individual clients are in order to help them make the most informed and beneficial decision. Some people need income today, while others need it in five or 10 years. Others may have their income needs met but are planning to move closer to their children and will need to buy a house in 10 years. Or, if you want income in 15 years, you might want to choose a different investment product for 10 years, and then switch to an annuity with an income rider during the last five years of your timeline. Everyone's situation is different and everyone's needs are different.

People who are interested in annuities, however, usually need to make decisions that affect their income needs, whether it is filling their income gap, or providing for income down the road. Many life insurance products today also offer attractive options for funding the costs of long-term care. Annuity products with critical-care riders or penalty-free options for healthcare expenses can be one of the keys to a good income plan. Other options include life insurance policies with chronic and terminal illness care, known as Living Benefit riders.

SINGLE PREMIUM IMMEDIATE ANNUITIES (SPIA)

What happens if you place on a shorter timeframe those assets from which you need to draw an income? Something called single premium immediate annuities may be for you.

A Single Premium Immediate Annuity (SPIA) is simply a contract between you and an insurance company. SPIAs are structured so that you pay a lump sum of money (a single premium) to an insurance company, and they give you a guaranteed income over an agreed upon time period. That time period could be five years, or it could be for the remainder of your lifetime. Guarantees from insurance companies are based on the claims-paying ability of the issuing insurance company.

SPIAs provide investors with a stream of reliable income when they can't afford to take the risk of losing money in a fluctuating market. While there is general faith that the market always trends up, at least in the long-term, if you are focusing on income over a shorter period of time, you may not be able to take a big hit in the market. Beyond normal market volatility, interest rates also come with an inherent level of uncertainty, making it hard to create a dependable income on your own. SPIAs reduce risk for you by giving you regular monthly, quarterly or yearly payments that can begin the moment you buy the contract. Your financial professional can walk you through a series of different payment options to help you select the one that most closely fits your needs.

Additional Annuity Information:
- Some contracts will allow you to draw income from the high water mark that the market reaches each year. The income rider will then begin calculating its value from the high water mark.
- Income annuities are investment tools that look and feel a bit like Social Security. Every year you allow the money to grow with the market, and it will "roll up" by a specific amount, paying out a specific percent to you as income each year.
- Annuities can work very well to create income. A financial professional can help you find the one that best matches your income need, and can also structure it to work perfectly for you.

Managing Risk Within Your Annuity:
Just like any investment strategy, the amount of risk needs to fit the comfort level of the investor. Annuities are no exception. Without going into too much detail, here are some additional ways to manage risk with annuity options:
- If you want to structure an annuity investment for growth over a long period of time, you can select a variable annuity. The value of your principal investment follows the market and can lose or gain value with the market. This type of annuity can also have an income rider, but it is really more useful as an accumulation tool that bets on an improving market. A 40-year-old couple, for example, will probably want to structure more for growth and take on more risk than someone in their 70s. The 40-year-old couple may select a variable annuity with an income rider

that kicks in when they plan to retire. If it rises with the market or outperforms it, the value of their investment has grown. If the market loses ground over the duration of the contract or their annuity underperforms, they can still rely on the income rider.

- If you are 68 years old and you have more immediate income needs that you need to come up with above and beyond your Social Security, you need a low risk, reliable source of income. If you choose an annuity option, you are looking for something that will pay out an income right away over a relatively short timeframe. You probably want to opt for a SPIA that pays you immediately and spans a five year period, as well as an additional annuity that begins paying you in five years, and another longer term annuity that begins paying you in 10 years. Bear in mind that each annuity contract has its own costs and fees. Review these with your financial professional before you determine the best products and strategies for your situation.

The following examples show just how helpful an indexed annuity option can be for a retiree:

> » *Mike and Betty are 62 years old and have decided to run the numbers to see what their retirement is going to look like. They know they currently need $6,000 per month to pay their bills and maintain their current lifestyle. They have also done their Social Security homework and have determined that, between the two of them, they will receive $4,200 per month in benefits. They also receive $350 per month in rent from a tenant who lives in a small carriage house in their backyard.*

Between their Social Security and the monthly rent income, they will be short $1,450 per month.

They do have an additional asset, however. They have been contributing for years to an IRA that has reached a value of $350,000. They realize that they have to figure out how to turn the $350,000 in their IRA into $1,450 per month for the rest of their life. At first glance, it may seem like they will have plenty of money. With some quick calculations, they find they have 240 months, or nearly 20 years, of monthly income before they exhaust the account. When you consider income tax, the potential for higher taxes in the future, and market fluctuations (because many IRAs are invested in the market), the amount in the IRA seems to have a little less clout. Every dollar Mike and Betty take out of the IRA is subject to income tax, and if they leave the remainder in the IRA, they run the risk of losing money in a volatile market. Once they retire and stop getting a paycheck every two weeks, they also stop contributing to their IRA. And when they aren't supplementing its growth with their own money, they are entirely dependent on market growth. That's a scary prospect. They could also withdraw the money from the IRA and put it in a savings account or CD, but removing all the money at once will put them in a tax bracket that will claim a huge portion of the value of the IRA. A seemingly straightforward asset has now become a complicated equation. Mike and Betty didn't know what to do, so they met with their financial professional.

Their financial professional suggested that they use the money to purchase an indexed annuity with an income rider. They selected an annuity that was designed for their specific situation. They took the lump sum from their IRA, placed it in an indexed annuity taking advantage of annual reset so they never lost the value of their investment. In return, they were guaranteed the $1,450 of income per month that they *needed to meet their retirement goals. The simplicity of the contract allowed them to do an analysis with their professional just once to understand the product. They basically put their money in an investment crockpot where they didn't have to look at it or manage it. They just needed to let it simmer. In fact, their professional was able to find an annuity for them that allowed them their $1,450 monthly payment with a lump sum of $249,455, leaving them more than $100,000 to reinvest somewhere else. Keep in mind that annuities are tax deferred, meaning you will pay tax on the income you receive from an annuity in the year you receive it.*

» Lorraine is 60 years old and is wondering how she can use her assets to provide her with a retirement income. She has a $5,000 per month income need. If she starts withdrawing her Social Security benefit in six years at age 66, it will provide her with $2,200 per month. She also has a pension that kicks in at age 70 that will give her another $1,320 per month.

That leaves an income gap of $2,800 from ages 66 to 69, and then an income gap of $1,480 at age 70 and beyond. If Lorraine uses only Yellow Money to solve her income need, she will need to deposit $918,360 at 2 percent interest to meet her monthly goal for her lifetime. If she opts to use Red Money and withdraws the amount she needs each month from the market, let's say the S & P 500, she will run out of cash in 10 years if she invested between the years of 2000 and 2012. Suffering a market downturn like that during the period for which she is relying on it for retirement income will change her life, and not for the better.

Working with a financial professional to find a better way, Lorraine found that she could take a hybrid approach to fill her income gap. Her professional recommended two different income vehicles: one that allowed her to deposit *just $190,161 with a 2 percent return, and one that was a $146,000 income annuity. These tools filled her income gap with $336,161, requiring her to spend $582,000 less money to accomplish her goal! Working with a professional to find the right tools for her retirement needs saved Lorraine over half a million dollars.*

ANNUITY INCOME STREAMS

Creating an income plan before you retire allows you to satisfy your need for lifetime income and ensures that your lifestyle can last as long as you do. You also want to create a plan that operates in the most efficient way possible. Doing so will give more security to your Need Later Money and will potentially allow you to build your legacy down the road.

Creating your own pension includes the following steps:

- Review your income needs and look specifically at the shortfall you may have during each year of your retirement based on your Social Security income, and income from any other assets you have.
- Ask yourself where you are in your distribution phase. Is retirement one year away? 10 years away? Last year?
- Determine how much money you need and how you need to structure your existing assets to provide for that need.
- If you have an asset from which you need to generate income, consider options offered by purchasing an income rider on an annuity.

» *Diane wants to retire at age 68. However, after her Social Security benefit, she will need nearly $375,000 in assets to generate a modest $40,000 of income per year.*

Amazingly, most people don't look ahead to think that at 68 years old, they will need $375,000 to have a basic lifestyle that pays out around $40,000 with Social Security benefits.

CHAPTER 6 RECAP //

- After Social Security and your additional income is accounted for, the amount that's still needed to meet your needs is called the *Income Gap*. It's important to consider future expense when planning for your income needs because most retirees will live longer than their parents did.

- Many retirees struggle to find the right investment tools during their retirement years. Typical interest rates on Yellow Money assets don't earn enough to keep pace with inflation and taxes, while money left in the market can potentially devastate your retirement income.

- Today's new annuities are designed to protect your retirement savings in any market. Annuities with income riders are designed to give you lifetime income. That income can go up in value as you wait to trigger a monthly check.

- Although an annuity is an income-producing asset that does not subject your income to market risk, it still has the opportunity to grow. An FIA is a Fixed Indexed Annuity, previously known as an EIA or Equity Indexed Annuity, is a special type of annuity that is keyed to the performance of the stock market. It offers growth with a guaranteed safety of your principal.

- The benefits of an FIA include: guarantee of principal, a minimum guaranteed cash value, no fees, access to your money, potential bonus money, tax deferral, and a guaranteed lifetime income.

- Be sure you understand the features, benefits, costs and fees associated with any annuity product before you invest.

7

What Else Can Go Wrong?

"Rule number one: Don't lose money.
Rule number two: Never forget rule number one."
~ Warren Buffet

Mike and Angela have a two-week road trip planned to the Grand Canyon. They have their route picked out and their hotels booked. They've got their suitcases packed, a cat sitter arranged and someone who will come to water the lawn. "We're all set," Mike says. "We've got everything planned." He takes one last look at the roadmap and then folds it up. His wife looks over, punches him in the side and says in a gentle, loving way, "Honey, have you had the car checked out?"

Angela in our story above is thinking about all the things that could go wrong on the way to the Grand Canyon. She is thinking about risk. What if the car breaks down? What if they lose their credit cards? Or what if one of them gets sick along the way? Thinking about all these "what ifs" might sound like a recipe for a sleepless night, but when it comes to retirement planning, the opposite is actually the case. The more you plan for the things that can go wrong, the better you sleep. Why? Because the question of whether or not things will go differently than planned isn't a case of *if* but *when.* In real life just as when planning trips, things never go *exactly* the way we think they will. Something always comes up.

Once your income needs are taken care of, it's time to take a look at other risk factors that can undermine your plan. During the 10 to 30 year timespan known as the golden years, there are a myriad of things that could come up. Not all of these potential problems require the purchase of an investment product. Sometimes, the solution is a strategy or a plan. However you solve these potential risks, having a conversation about them at least puts everything on the table where you can look at what's what. Knowing you've taken the time to address these issues goes a long way toward achieving greater peace of mind so you can sleep soundly during your retirement years.

HAVE YOU CONSIDERED THE OTHER RISKS?

There are several risks specific to your retirement years that you don't have to think about as seriously during other stages of your life. Preparing for these risks will greatly increase the chances that you get to where you are going and achieve your retirement goals. Not only do you need to secure your assets and coordinate an income that you can rely on, you also need to consider other things that can go wrong and have a major impact on you during your retirement years. When you plan for a trip, you take preventative measures such as giving the car a tune-up or an oil change, checking the spare and maybe replacing the wiper blades. You make copies of your credit cards and secure emergency funds. You do a little bit of buying and a little bit of planning to make sure things are in place for a happy outcome. Planning for retirement requires the same kind of proactive thinking. What follows is by no means a comprehensive list of all the things that can go wrong, but it covers the basics.

Risk #1: Longevity Risk: Thanks to a healthier lifestyle and medical advances, most seniors today are living longer and stronger into their retirement years. Not only are we living longer, but our life expectancy actually increases the older we get. According to the Society of Actuaries 2000 Mortality Table, a couple that makes it to age 65 has a 99 percent chance of living into their 70s, and a 94 percent chance of living into their 80s. That means you need to plan for what your needs may be at that point in your life.

Risk #2: Health Care Costs: The rising costs of health care, when combined with longevity can quickly drain your retirement savings if not planned for properly. According to Genworth Financial's 2010 Cost of Care Survey, your health care expenses as a retiree could exceed $400,000 over the course of 20 years. When you consider your chances of living another 20 years, it makes sense to create a plan that addresses this reality.

Risk #3: Personal or Event Risk: Family issues often create a surprising risk to retirement savings. If your son or daughter goes through a divorce and asks you for money to help on the down payment of a house in a safe neighborhood for the grandkids, and you have that money sitting in an IRA, can you say no? Most people find that they cannot. Having a plan in place to help take care of the people you love prevents tax consequences and risk to the assets you need to rely on for income during your retirement.

Risk #4: Cost Of Long Term Care: Statistics reveal that 70 percent of retirees age 65 today will need some form of long term care, and 20 percent of those cases will require care for five years or longer.* If these expenses are planned for ahead of time, you will have a lot more options when it comes to paying for them using your retirement money. Keep in mind, your strategy may or may NOT include purchasing a Long Term Care policy. Begin with a strategy, then find the right tool.

Risk #5: Premature Death of a Spouse: Nobody wants to think about the possibility of losing a spouse, but what if it happens to you? Will your income stay the same, or will there be a reduction? If one of you receives a large pension, and that pension disappears, how will you pay the bills? Spousal continuation factors into whether that income is guaranteed or not. Look at all your other options to make sure you are both taken care of in the event of death. And remember, if you're both receiving Social Security benefits, at the death of one spouse the smaller of the two benefits will go away. Plan on it!

Risk #6: Another Market downturn: We've talked about market risk throughout the book but in case you need a refresher, managing your money according to the 1-2-3's of conservative investing is one way to manage this risk. You can't control the return on your assets, but you do control where those assets are invested and at what risk. Our motto: you can't manage returns, only risk.

Risk #7: Inflation: Year in and year out, inflation erodes the purchasing power of your retirement savings. $1,000 saved today and adjusted for inflation (assuming a 4 percent annual rate of inflation) will amount to only $822 in 5 years, and a mere $675 in 10 years. You can't control inflation, which means there has to be some participation in the market. Managed money can be one way to mitigate this risk. We will talk more about this option in the next chapter entitled, "What is Orange Money?"

*http://longtermcare.gov/the-basics/how-much-care-will-you-need/

Risk #8: Taxes: For most people, the vast majority of their future income is going to be taxable. Pension plans are 100 percent taxable; 401(k)s, 403(b)s and traditional IRAs are also fully taxable at the individual's income tax rate. There are a number of strategies that can help you minimize the effect of taxes or even avoid some taxes altogether. The first step will be to review your previous year's tax return with an eye for missed deductions. The Internal Revenue Service tax code has grown to 71,000 pages as of 2010, making working with a tax professional an invaluable tool to ensure you don't pay more taxes than you have to. Additionally, there are several strategies available to reduce future taxes on qualified holdings, as well as Social Security benefits.

What will you be doing during your retirement years? Traveling? Starting a business? Enjoying the grandkids? Preparing for all the risks that come with the territory will help you lay the ground work for the living roadmap that can take you to the destination of your retirement dreams.

PAYING FOR EMERGENCIES: A DISCUSSION ABOUT LIQUIDITY

In Chapter 1, we discussed how today's investment options requires advice that is relevant to today. Traditional, outdated investment strategies are not only ineffective; they can be harmful to the average investor. One of the most traditional ways of thinking about investing is the risk versus reward trade-off. It goes something like this.

Investment options that are considered safer carry less risk, but also offer the potential for less return. Riskier investment options carry the burden of volatility and a greater potential for loss, but they also offer a greater potential for large rewards. Most professionals move their clients back and forth along this range, shifting between investments that are safer and investments that are structured for growth. Essentially, the old rules of investing dictate that you can either choose relative safety *or* return, but you can't have both.

Updated investment strategies work with the flexibility of liquidity to remake the rules. Here is how:

There are three dimensions that are inherent in any investment: *Liquidity, Safety,* and *Return*. You can maximize any two of these dimensions at the expense of the third. If you choose Safety and Liquidity, this is like keeping your assets in a checking account or savings account. This option delivers a lot of Safety and Liquidity, but at the expense of any Return. On the other hand, if you choose Liquidity and Return, meaning you have the potential for great return and can still reclaim your money whenever you choose, you will likely be exposed to a very high level of risk.

As this relates to the 1-2-3's of conservative investing, you can look at your investments according to their color to see exactly where they stand with regards to liquidity, safety and return.

- *Yellow Money*: liquidity plus safety, but no significant return.
- *Red Money*: liquidity plus return, but no safety.
- *Green Money*: return with safety, but some loss of liquidity.

Understanding Liquidity can help you break the old Risk versus Safety trade-off. By identifying assets which don't require Liquidity, you can place yourself in a position to potentially profit from relatively safe investments that provide a higher than average rate of return when planning for Need Later Money and expenses that might crop up later.

Choosing Safety and Return over Liquidity can have significant impacts on the accumulation of your assets. In Lane's case, the paradigm shift from earning and saving to leveraging assets was a costly one.

» *Lane is a corn and soybean farmer with 1,200 acres of land. He routinely retains somewhere between $40,000 and $80,000 in his checking and savings accounts. If a major piece of equipment fails and needs repair or replacement, he will need the money available to pay for the equipment and carry on with farming. If the price of feed for his cattle goes up one year, he will need to compensate for the increased overhead to his farming operation. He isn't a particularly wealthy farmer, but he has little choice but to keep a portion of money on hand in case something comes up and he must access it quickly. Most of his capital is held in livestock in the pasture or crops in the ground tied up for six to eight months of the year. When a major financial need arises, Lane can't just harvest 10 acres of soybeans and use them for payment. He needs to depend heavily on Liquidity in order to be a successful farmer.*

Old habits die hard, however, and when Lane finally hangs up his overalls and quits farming, he keeps his bank accounts flush with cash, just like in the old days. After selling the farm and the equipment, Lane keeps a huge portion of the profits in Liquid investments because that's what he is familiar with. Unfortunately for Lane, with his pile of money sitting in his checking account, he isn't even keeping pace with inflation. After all his hard work as a farmer, his money is losing value every day because he didn't shift to a paradigm of leveraging his assets to generate income and accumulate value.

Almost anything would be a better option for Lane than clinging to Liquidity. He could have done something better to get either more return from his money or more safety, and at the very least would not have lost out to inflation.

As you can see, Yellow Money has its own kind of built-in penalty—that of earning a low to zero rate of return. You want to have enough Liquidity to pay for emergency expenses that crop up, but you don't want to have all of your money there. When growing a portion of your money for Need Later funds, the sooner you want your money back, the less you can leverage it for Safety or Return. If you have the option of putting your money in a long-term investment, you will be sacrificing Liquidity, but potentially gaining both Safety and Return. Rethinking your approach to money in this way can make a world of difference and can provide you with a structured way to generate income while allowing the value of your asset to grow over time.

How much Liquidity do you _really_ need? Think about it. If you haven't sat down and created an income plan for your retirement, your perceived need for Liquidity is a guess. You don't know how much cash you'll need to fill the income gap if you don't know the amount of your Social Security benefit or the total of your other income options. If you have determined your income needs and have made a plan for filling your income gap, you can now partition your assets based on when you will need them. An income plan that includes both Need Now and Need Later Money can use new rules, strategies and investment tools so you can enjoy both Safety and Return from your assets, _and_ have access to the cash when you need it.

THE BUCKET STRATEGY: WHAT'S IT FOR AND WHEN DO I NEED IT?

One very successful strategy used for combating the risk of Need Later money is known as laddering. Laddering simply means you separate your accumulation buckets from the buckets of money you rely on for producing income. Why would you do this? Separate buckets allow you to use Yellow, Red and Green Money investments to capture the best of all three, Liquidity, Safety and Return.

This strategy works by using multiple investment tools, or buckets, each assigned for a purpose and set to grow at different time periods. Each bucket is assigned a risk value according to its purpose. This way you know exactly what money to use and when to use it so as to maximize every dollar. This strategy satisfies your need for income and incorporates tax considerations and future money needs.

An example:

- *Bucket #1*: Yellow money for today's needs. This is money in your checking or savings account, used for paying today's bills.
- *Bucket #2*: This is also Yellow Money set aside in a savings account or a money market account earmarked for emergency funds that you may tap into once or twice a year.
- *Buckets #3 and #4*: These are Green Money income buckets designed for producing a steady stream of guaranteed income. You might have one or multiple Green Money buckets depending on the strategy you are using here.
- *Buckets #5 and up*: These are Orange or Red Money buckets designed for growing your money for needs that are 10, 15, or even 30 years down the road. We will talk about Orange Money in the next chapter entitled, "What is Orange Money?"

Taking control of your assets and protecting your nest egg is where the muscle of your plan really goes to work for you. As you set your plan into motion, it's important to revisit the plan at least annually. Your financial professional should stay in touch with you to make adjustments, re-strategize, and fine-tune your plan as life events such as weddings, births, divorce, and new cars come into play. When these life events crop up, it's important to pull the needed funds from the right account in order to avoid costly mistakes to your nest egg assets.

Having a strategy in place for life's problems big and small means you can use today's products and new rules to get the best of both Safety and Return from your retirement assets.

CHAPTER 7 RECAP //

- Planning right means taking into consideration all the risk factors that affect your retirement savings including longevity, inflation, taxes, health care, personal events and spousal continuation.
- The three aspects of any investment include liquidity, safety, and return. You can choose to maximize any two against the third. Or you can use strategies that combine Yellow, Green and Red Money investment tools designed for today's retirees and work with a financial professional. With the right tools and strategies, it is possible to achieve aspects of all three, Liquidity, Safety and Return.
- Choosing to maximize liquidity alone can be an expensive option because the sooner you need your money back, the less you can leverage it for safety and return.
- To plan for a successful retirement in today's economy requires a creative use of strategies and today's financial tools.

8

What is Orange Money?

When Mark was a kid, he used to amaze all his friends with his prophetic abilities. He had a Magic Eight Ball he kept in his pocket and whenever someone wanted to know something such as, "Will I fail my math test?" Mark would take out that Magic Eight Ball, give it a shake, and announce his prophecy according to the Eight Ball: "It doesn't look good for you." And everybody would have a good laugh.

Flash-forward in time and Mark is still using his Magic Eight Ball. He now works as a financial professional and whenever someone asks him what the stock market will do, he says, "Oh, well I have this Magic Eight Ball." He takes it out of his drawer, gives it a shake, and comes up with an answer:

"Ask again later!" "As I see it, yes!" "Concentrate and ask again!" "Without a doubt!" "You may rely on it!" And, "My reply is No."

If you ask someone what the market is going to do, they will tell you the story they want to tell you based on who is paying them, or what's in it for them. We all know that magic eight-balls aren't magic, they are just for fun, and yet there might be some professionals out there who claim to have actual prophetic abilities. We will talk more about this later under the heading, Stock Broker vs RIA, but for now, we're going to address the question: How can you do a better job with your Red Money assets? How can you increase the chances that it will grow to cover your Need Later Money needs and help pay for the risks that are coming down the road? How can you do this without using magic tricks? The answer is actively managed money.

INTRODUCING ORANGE MONEY

The foundation of your retirement income comes from your Green Money. Now that you've calculated the Rule of 100, determined how much risk you have and how much you want, and determined how much Green and Yellow Money you need to meet your short-term needs, it's time to look at what you have left. The money you have left after you've calculated your needs has the potential of becoming Red Money: your stocks, mutual funds, precious metals and other investment products that you want to continue accumulating value within the markets. You now have the luxury of taking a closer second look at your Red Money to determine how you would like to manage it.

As you read earlier in the key findings of the DALBAR report, the deck is stacked against the individual investor. Remember that the average investor on a fixed income failed to keep pace with inflation in nine of the last 14 years, meaning the inherent risk in managing your Red Money is very real and could have a lasting impact on your assets. So, how much of your Red Money do you invest, and in what kinds of markets, investment products and stocks do you invest? There are a lot of different directions in which you can take your Red Money. One thing is for sure: significant growth depends on investing in the market. How you go about doing it is different for everyone. Gathering stocks, bonds and investment funds together in a portfolio without a cohesive strategy behind them could cause you to miss out on the benefits of a more thoughtful and planned approach. The end result is that you may never really understand what your money is doing, where and how it is really invested, and which investment principles are behind the investment products you hold. While you may have goals for each individual piece of your portfolio, it is likely that you don't have a comprehensive plan for your Red Money, which may mean that *you are taking on more risk than you would like, and are getting less return for it than is possible.*

Enter Orange Money. Orange Money is Red Money that is managed by a professional *with a purpose.* After your income needs are met and you have assets that you would like to dedicate to accumulation, there are decisions you need to make about how to invest those assets. You can buy stocks, index funds, mutual funds, bonds — you name it — you can invest in it. The difference between Red Money and Orange Money is that Orange Money has a cohesive strategy behind it that is *implemented by a professional.* When you manage your Red Money with an investment plan, it becomes Orange Money: *money that is being managed with a specific purpose, a specific set of focused goals and a specific written strategy of when to buy and sell in mind.*

Orange Money is still a type of Red Money. It comes with different levels of risk. But Orange Money is under the watchful eye of professionals who have a stake in the success of your money in the market and who can recommend a range of strategies from those designed for preservation to those targeting rapid growth. You don't want to miss out on achieving the right level of risk, and more importantly, composing a careful plan for the return of your assets.

It can be helpful to think of Orange Managed Money with this analogy: Imagine a loaded pistol sitting on a coffee table in the middle of a room. This room is filled with people—babies, kids, teenagers and adults—but none of them know how to use a gun. Still they are curious. They might pick it up and see what it can do. Is the gun dangerous? That gun, unattended and unmanaged, is like Red Money.

Take that same loaded pistol and now, put it into the hands of a trained professional. This person knows how to use the gun, when to put it in the holster, when to draw it, and when to put the safety on or take it off. They also know when to pull the trigger—which in this context, translates to selling an investment. A gun, when in the hands of a professional, becomes a tool. Red Money, in the hands of a professional, can also become a tool and this is why we label managed money as Orange Money.

TAKING A CLOSER LOOK AT YOUR PORTFOLIO

Think about your investment portfolio. Think specifically of what you would consider your Red Money. Do you know what is there? You may have several different investment products like individual mutual funds, bond accounts, stocks, etc. You may have inherited a stock portfolio from a relative, or you might be invested in a bond account offered by the company for which you worked due to your familiarity with them. While you may or may not be managing your investments individually, the reality is that you probably don't have an overall management strategy for all of your investments. Investments that aren't managed are simply Red Money, or money that is at risk in the market.

Harnessing the earning potential of your Red Money relies on more than a collection of stocks and bonds, however. It needs guided management. A good Orange Money manager uses the knowledge they have about the level of risk with which you are comfortable, what you need or want to use your money for, when you want or need it and how you want to use it. The Orange Money objects that they choose for you will still have a certain level of risk, but under the right management, control and process, you have a far better chance of a successful outcome that meets your specific needs.

When you sit down with an investment professional, you can look at all of your assets together. Chances are that you have accumulated a number of different assets over the last 20, 30 or 50 years. You may have a 401(k), an IRA, a Roth IRA, an account of self-directed stocks, a brokerage account, etc. Wherever you put your money, a financial professional will go through your assets and help you determine the level of risk to which you are exposed now and should be exposed in the future.

Here is a typical example of how an investment professional can be helpful to a future retiree with Orange Money needs:

> *Janet is 65 years old and wants to retire in two years. She has a 401(k) from her job to which she has contributed for 26 years. She also has some stocks that her late husband managed. Janet also has $55,000 in a mutual fund that her sister recommended to her five years ago and $30,000 in another mutual fund that she heard about at work. She takes a look at her assets one day and decides that she doesn't understand what they add up to or what kind of retirement they will provide. She decides to meet with an investment professional. Janet's professional immediately asks her:*

> *1. **Does she know exactly where all of her money is?** Janet doesn't know much about all her husband's stocks, which have now become hers. Their value is at $100,000 invested in three large cap companies. Janet is unsure of the companies and whether she should hold or sell them.*

> *2. **Does she know what types of assets she owns?** Yes and no. She knows she has a 401(k) and IRAs, but she is*

unfamiliar with her husband's self-directed stock portfolio or the type of mutual funds she owns. Furthermore she is unclear as to how to manage the holdings as she nears retirement.

3. Does she know the strategies behind each one of the investment products she owns? *While Janet knows she has a 401(k), an IRA and mutual fund holdings, she doesn't know how her 401(k) is organized or how to make it more conservative as she nears retirement. She is unsure whether her IRA is a Roth or traditional variety and how to draw income from them. She really does not have specific investment principles guiding her investment decisions, and she certainly doesn't have a plan as to when to buy or sell. One other major concern for Janet is whether her family would be okay if she were not around?*

After determining Janet's assets, her financial professional prepares a consolidated report that lays out all of her assets for her to review. Her professional explains each one of them to her. Janet discovers that although she is two years away from retiring, her 401(k) is organized with an amount of risk with which she is not comfortable. Sixty percent of her 401(k) is at risk, far off the mark if we abide by the Rule of 100. Janet opts to be more conservative than the Rule of 100 suggests, as she will rely on her 401(k) for most of her immediate income needs after retirement. Janet's professional also points out several instances of overlap between her mutual funds. Janet learns that while she is comfortable with one of her mutual funds, she does not agree with the management principles of the other. In the end, Janet's professional helps her reorganize her 401(k) to secure her more Green Money for retirement income. Her professional also uses her mutual fund and her husband's stock assets to create a growth oriented investment plan that Janet will rely on for Need Later Money in 15 years when she plans on relocating closer to her children and grandchildren. By creating an overall investment strategy, Janet is able to meet her targeted goals in retirement. Finally, Janet's financial professional worked closely with her and her tax professional to minimize the tax impact of any asset sales in Janet's situation.

Like Janet, you may have several savings vehicles: a 401(k), an IRA to which you regularly contribute, some mutual funds to which you make monthly contributions, etc. But what is your *overall investment strategy?* Do you have one in place? Do you want one that will help you meet your retirement goals? Orange Money looks at *ALL* your accounts and all their different strategies to create a plan that helps them all work together. Your current investment situation may not reflect your wishes. As a matter of fact, it likely doesn't.

You may have a better understanding of your assets than Janet did, but even someone with an investment strategy can benefit from having a financial professional review their portfolio:

> » *Oscar is 69 years old. He retired four years ago. He relied on income from an IRA for three years in order to increase his Social Security benefit. He also made significant investments in 36 different mutual funds. He chose to diversify among the funds by selecting a portion for growth, another for good dividends, another that focused on promising small cap companies and a final portion that work like index funds. All the money that Oscar had in mutual funds he considered Need Later Money that he wanted to rely on in his 80s. After the stock market took a hit in 2008, Oscar lost some confidence in his investments and decided to sit down with a financial professional to see if his portfolio was able to recover.*

The professional Oscar met with was able to determine what goals he had in mind. Specifically, the financial professional determined what Oscar actually wanted and needed the money for, and when he needed it. His professional also looked inside each of the mutual funds and discovered several instances of overlap. While Oscar had created diversity in his portfolio by selecting funds focused on different goals, he didn't account for overlap in the companies in which the funds were invested. Out of the 36 funds, his professional found that 20 owned nearly identical stock. While most of the companies were good investments, the high instance of overlap did not contribute to the healthy investment diversity that Oscar wanted. Oscar's financial professional also provided him with a report that explained the concentration ratio of his holdings (noting how much of his portfolio was contained within the top 25 stock holdings), the percentage of his portfolio that each company he invested in represented (showing the percentage of net assets that each company made up as an overall position in his portfolio) and the portfolio date of his account (showing when the funds in his portfolio were last updated: as funds are required to report updates only twice per year, it was possible that some of his fund reports could be six months old).

Oscar's professional consolidated his assets into one investment management strategy. This allowed Oscar's investments to be managed by someone he trusted who knew his specific investment goals and needs. Eliminating redundancy and overlap in his portfolio was easy to do but difficult to detect since Oscar had multiple funds with multiple brokerage firms. Oscar sat down with a professional to see if his mutual funds could perform well, and he left with a consolidated management plan and an active money manager that understood him personally. That's Orange Money at its best.

But true active management of assets goes one step further. There are now available, even for somewhat smaller accounts down to $50,000, managed accounts that utilize signals in the market to move in and out. These accounts primarily use ETF's because of their low cost and sellability, but stocks can also be used.

By using signals, portfolio managers are able to avoid severe dips in the market and take advantage in buying back in at close to the right point. This is not to say that it is perfect, but the track record on some of the most notable money managers is quite impressive.

Another positive? No commissions. Many financial professionals are paid via fees based on a percentage of the size of the account. If the account makes money, the investor makes money and the financial professional makes money. It's a win-win!

AVOIDING EMOTIONAL INVESTING

There's no way around it; people get emotional about their money. And for good reason. You've spent your life working for it, exchanging your time and talent for it, and making decisions about how to invest it, save it and make it grow. The maintenance of your lifestyle and your plans for retirement all depend on it. The best investment strategies, however, don't rely on emotions. One of Orange Money's greatest strengths lies in the fact that it is managed by someone who understands your needs and desires, but doesn't make decisions about your money under the influence of emotion.

A well-managed investment account meets your goals as a whole, not in individualized and piecemeal ways. Professional money managers do this by creating requirements for each type of investment in which they put your money. We'll call them "screens." Your money manager will run your holdings through the screens they have created to evaluate different types of investment strategies. A professionally managed account will only have holdings that meet the requirements laid out in the overall management plan that was designed to meet your investment goals. The holdings that don't make it through the screens, the ones that don't contribute to your investment goals, are sold and redistributed to investments that your financial professional has determined to be appropriate.

Different screens apply to different Orange Money strategies. For example, if one of your goals is significant growth, which would require taking on more risk alongside the potential for more return, an investment professional would screen for companies that have high rates of revenue and sales growth, high earnings growth, rising profit margins, and innovative products. On the other hand, if you want your portfolio to be used for income, which would call for lower risk and less return, your professional would screen for dividend yield and sector diversification. *Every investor has a different goal, and every goal requires a customized strategy that uses quantitative screens.* A professional will create a portfolio that reflects your investment desires. If some of the current assets you own complement the strategies that your professional recommends, those will likely stay in your portfolio.

Screening your assets removes emotions from the equation. It removes attachment to underperforming or overly risky investments. Financial professionals aren't married to particular stocks or mutual funds for any reason. They go by the numbers and see your portfolio through a lens shaped by your retirement goals. Your professional understands your wants and needs, and creates an investment strategy that takes your life events and future plans into account. It's a planful approach, and it allows you to tap into the tools and resources of a professional who has built a career around successful investing. Managing money is a full-time job and is best left to a professional money manager.

Removing emotions from investing also allows you to be unaffected by the day-to-day volatility of the market so that you can enjoy a worry-free retirement with peace of mind. Your financial professional doesn't ask where the market is going to be in a year, three years or a month from now. If you look at the value of the stock market from the beginning of the twentieth century to today, it's going up. Despite the Great Depression, despite the 1987 crash, despite the 2008 market downturn, the market, as a whole, trends up. Remember the major market downturn in 2008 when the market lost 30 percent of its value? Not only did it completely recover, it has far exceeded its 2008 value. Emotional investing led countless people to sell low as the market went down, and buy the same shares back when the market started to recover. That's an expensive way to do business. While you can't afford to lose money that you need in two, three or five years, your Need Later Money has time to grow. The best way to accomplish this is to make it Orange.

CREATING AN INVESTMENT STRATEGY

Just like Janet and Oscar, chances are that you can benefit from taking a more managed investment approach tailored to your goals. Orange Money is generally Need Later Money that you want to grow for needs you'll have in at least 10 years. You can work with your financial planner to create investments that meet your needs within different timeframes. You may need to rely on some of your Orange Money in 10, 15 or 20 years, whether for additional income, a large purchase you plan on making or a vacation. Whatever you want it for, you will need it down the road. A financial professional can help you rescale the risk of your assets as they grow, helping you lock in your profits and secure a source of income you can depend on later.

So what does an Orange Money account look like? Here's what it *doesn't* look like: a portfolio with 49 small cap mutual funds, a dozen individual stocks and an assortment of bond accounts. A brokerage account with a hodgepodge of investments, even if goal-oriented, is not a professionally managed account. It's still Red Money. Remember, an Orange Money account has an overarching investment philosophy. When you look at making investments that will perform to meet your future income needs, the burning question becomes: How much should you have in the market and how should it be invested? Working with a professional will help you determine how much risk you should take, how to balance your assets so they will meet your goals and how to plan for the big ticket items, like health care expenses, that may be in your future. Yes, Orange Money is exposed to risk, but by working with a professional, you can manage that risk in a productive way.

WHY ORANGE MONEY?

If you have met your immediate income needs for retirement, why bother with professionally managing your other assets? The money you have accumulated above and beyond your income needs probably has a greater purpose. It may be for your children or grandchildren. You may want to give money to a charity or organization that you admire. In short, you may want to craft your legacy. It would be advantageous to grow your assets in the best manner possible. A financial professional has built a career around managing money in profitable ways. They are experts under the supervision of the organization that they represent.

Turning to Orange Money also means that you don't have to burden yourself with the time commitment, the stress, and the cost of determining how to manage your money. Orange Money can help you better enjoy your retirement. Do you want to sit down in your home office every day and determine how to best allocate your assets, or do you want to be living your life while someone else manages your money for you? When the majority of your Red Money is managed with a specific purpose by a financial professional, you don't have to be worrying about which stocks to buy and sell today or tomorrow.

SEEKING FINANCIAL ADVICE: STOCK BROKERS VS. INVESTMENT ADVISOR REPRESENTATIVES

Investors basically have access to two types of advice in today's financial world: advice from stock brokers and advice given by investment advisors. Most investors, however, don't know the difference between types of advice and the people from whom they receive advice. Today, there are two primary types of advice offered to investors: advice given by a commission-based registered representative (brokers) and advice given by fee-based Investment Advisor Representatives. Unfortunately, many investors are not aware that a difference exists; nor have they been explained the distinction between the two types of advice. In a survey taken by TD Ameritrade, the top reasons investors choose to work with an independent registered investment advisor are:*

- Registered Investment Advisors are required, as fiduciaries, to offer advice that is in the best interest of clients
- More personalized service and competitive fee structure offered at a Registered Investment Advisor firm
- Dissatisfaction with full commission brokers

The truth is that there is a great deal of difference between stock brokers and investment advisor representatives. For starters, investment advisor representatives are obligated to act in an investor's best interests in every aspect of a financial relationship.

---

*2011 Advisor Sentiment Study, commissioned by TD AMERITRADE. TD Ameritrade, Inc.

Confusion continues to exist among investors struggling to find the best financial advice out there and the most credible sources of advice.

Here is some information to help clear up the confusion so you can find good advice from a professional you can trust:

- Investment advisor representatives have the fiduciary duty to act in a client's best interest at all times with every investment decision they make. Stock brokers and brokerage firms usually do not act as fiduciaries to their investors and are not obligated to make decisions that are entirely in the best interest of their customers. For example, if you decide you want to invest in precious metals, a stock broker would offer you a precious metals account from their firm. But an Investment Advisor would find you a precious metals account that is the best fit for you based on the investment strategy of your portfolio.

- Investment advisors give their clients a Form ADV describing the methods that the professional uses to do business. An Investment Advisor also obtains client consent regarding any conflicts of interest that could exist with the business of the professional. Stock brokers and brokerage firms *are not* obligated to provide comparable types of disclosure to their customers.

- Whereas stock brokers and firms routinely earn large profits by trading as principal with customers, Investment Advisors cannot trade with clients as principal (except in very limited and specific circumstances).

- Investment Advisors typically charge a pre-negotiated fee with their clients in advance of any transactions. They cannot earn additional profits or commissions from their customers' investments without prior consent. Registered Investment Advisors are commonly paid an asset-based fee that aligns their interests with those of their clients.

Brokerage firms and stock brokers, on the other hand, have much different payment agreements. Their revenues may increase regardless of the performance of their customers' assets.

- Unlike brokerage firms, where investment banking and underwriting are commonplace, Registered Investment Advisors must manage money in the best interests of their customers. Because Registered Investment Advisors charge set fees for their services, their focus is on their client. Brokerage firms may focus on other aspects of the firm that do not contribute to the improvement of their clients' assets.
- Unlike brokers, Registered Investment Advisors do not get commissions for selling funds or stock.

Just to drive home the point, here is what a fiduciary duty to a client means for a Registered Investment Advisor. Registered Investment Advisors must:*

- Always act in the best interest of their client and make investment decisions that reflect their goals.
- Identify and monitor securities that are illiquid.
- When appropriate, employ fair market valuation procedures.
- Observe procedures regarding the allocation of investment opportunities, including new issues and the aggregation of orders.
- Have policies regarding affiliated broker-dealers and maintenance of brokerage accounts.
- Disclose all conflicts of interest.

---

*2011 Advisor Sentiment Study, commissioned by TD AMERITRADE. TD Ameritrade, Inc.

- Have policies on use of brokerage commissions for research.
- Have policies regarding directed brokerage, including step-out trades and payment for order flow.
- Abide by a code of ethics.

CHAPTER 8 RECAP //

- Orange Money is money that is managed by a professional with a purpose. It is still considered a type of Red Money, but there is a dedicated direction, strategy and end-goal in mind, which makes it less dangerous.
- The risk of Red Money is like a loaded gun left in the middle of a crowded room. When you take that same gun and put it into the hands of a trained professional, the gun is no longer as dangerous. This same analogy applies to Red Money in the hands of a professional: it becomes Orange Money, because it is not as dangerous.
- Orange Money is managed without emotions. A financial professional manages the Orange Money using a specific criteria designed to fit into your overall financial plan so that it works the way you want it to.

9

Whose Retirement Money Is It?
Paying Taxes to Uncle Sam

Who is first in line to get your money?

George and Leslie, a 62-year-old couple, begin working with a financial professional in October. After structuring their assets to reflect their risk tolerance and creating assets that would provide them Green Money income during retirement, they feel good about their situation. They make decisions that allow them to maximize their Social Security benefits, they have plenty of options for filling their income gap, and have begun a safe yet ambitious Orange Money strategy with their professional. When their professional asks them about their tax plan, they tell him their CPA handled their taxes every year, and did a great job. Their professional says, "I don't mean who does your taxes, I mean, who does your tax planning?"

George and Leslie aren't sure how to respond.

Their professional brings George and Leslie's financial plan to the firm's tax planner and has her run a tax projection for them. A week later their professional calls them with a tax plan for the year that will save them more than $3,000 on their tax return. The couple is shocked. A simple piece of advice from the tax planner based on the numbers revealed that if they paid their estimated taxes before the end of the year, they would be able to itemize it as a deduction, allowing them to save thousands of dollars.

This solution won't work for everyone, and it may not work for George and Leslie every year. That's not the point. By being proactive with their approach to taxes and using the resources made available by their financial professional, they were able to create a tax plan that saved them money.

Tax planning **and** ***tax reporting*** **are two very different things**. Most people only *report* their taxes. March rolls around, people pull out their 1040s or use TurboTax to enter their income and taxable assets, and ship it off to the IRS. If you use a CPA to report your taxes, you are essentially paying them to record history. Doing your taxes in January, February, March or April means you are writing a history book. Planning your taxes in October, November or December means that you are writing the story as it happens. You can look at all the factors that are at play and make decisions that will impact your tax return *before* you file it.

Working with a financial professional who has expertise in proactive tax planning will keep you looking forward instead of in the rearview mirror as you enter retirement.

WHO IS FIRST IN LINE? UNCLE SAM AND YOUR RETIREMENT

You have the option of being proactive with your taxes and to plan for your future by making smart, informed decisions about how taxes affect your overall financial plan. When you retire, you move from the earning and accumulation phase of your life into the asset distribution phase of your life. For most people, that means relying on Social Security, a 401(k), an IRA, or a pension. Wherever you have put your Green Money for retirement, you are going to start relying on it to provide you with the income that once came as a paycheck. Most of these distributions will be considered income by the IRS and Uncle Sam will be standing by, waiting for his share. There are exceptions to that (not all of your Social Security income is taxed, and income from Roth IRAs is not taxed), but for the most part, your distributions are considered income and Uncle Sam will want his share.

Regarding assets that you have in an IRA or a 401(k) plan that uses an IRA, when you reach 70 ½ years of age, you will be required to draw a certain amount of money from your IRA as income each year. That amount depends on your age and the balance in your IRA. The amount that you are required to withdraw as income is called a Required Minimum Distribution (RMD). Why are you required to withdraw money from your own account? Chances are the money in that account has grown over time, and Uncle Sam wants to collect taxes on that growth. If you have a large balance in an IRA, there's a chance your RMD could increase your income significantly enough to put you into a higher tax bracket, subjecting you to a higher tax rate. This will make Uncle Sam happy, but how will you feel about it?

Here's where tax planning can really begin to work strongly in your favor. In the distribution phase of your life, you have a predictable income based on your RMDs, your Social Security benefit and any other income-generating assets you may have.

What really impacts you at this stage is how much of that money you keep in your pocket after taxes. Essentially, *you will make more money saving on taxes than you will by making more money.* If you can reduce your tax burden by 30, 20 or even 10 percent, you earn yourself that much more money by not paying it in taxes. In other words, the money goes into *your* wallet instead of into the hands of Uncle Sam.

How do you save money on taxes? *By having a plan.* In this instance, a financial professional that is experienced in tax planning can work with the CPAs at their firm to create a **distribution plan** that minimizes your taxes and maximizes your annual net income.

TAX MISTAKES AND HOW THEY IMPACT YOU

The average retirees are not looking to be multimillionaires. They are looking to retire comfortably, and they don't have thousands or even hundreds of dollars they consider expendable. This is why money mistakes that can easily be avoided are so troubling. The implications of proactive tax planning are far reaching, and are larger than many people realize. Remember, doing your taxes in January, February, March or April means you are writing a history book. Planning your taxes in October, November or December means that you are writing the story as it happens. You can look at all the factors that are at play and make decisions that will impact your tax return *before* you file it.

Realizing that tax planning is an aspect of financial planning is an important leap to make. When you incorporate tax planning into your financial planning strategy, it becomes part of the way you maximize your financial potential. Paying less in taxes means you keep more of your money. Simply put, the more money you keep, the more of it you can leverage as an asset. This kind of planning can affect you at any stage of your life. If you are 40 years old, are you contributing the maximum amount to your

401(k) plan? Are you contributing to a Roth IRA? Are you finding ways to structure the savings you are dedicating to your children's education? Do you have life insurance? Taxes and tax planning affects all of these investment tools. Having a relationship with a professional who works with a CPA can help you build a truly comprehensive financial plan that not only works with your investments, but also shapes your assets to find the most efficient ways to prepare for tax time. There may be years that you could benefit from higher distributions because of the tax bracket that you are in, or there could be years you would benefit from taking less. There may be years when you have a lot of deductions and years you have relatively few. **Adapting your distributions to work in concert with your available deductions** is at the heart of smart tax planning. Professional guidance can bring you to the next level of income distribution, allowing you to remain flexible enough to maximize your tax efficiency. And remember, saving money on taxes makes you more money than making money does.

What you have on paper is important: your assets, savings and investments, which are all financial expressions of your work and time. It's just as important to know how to get it off the paper in a way that keeps most of it in your pocket. Almost anything that involves financial planning also involves taxes. Annuities, investments, IRAs, 401(k)s, 403(b)s, and many other investment options will have tax implications. Life also has a way of throwing curveballs. Illness, expensive car repair or replacement, or *any event that has a financial impact on your life will likely have a corresponding tax implication* around which you should adapt your financial plan. Tax planning does just that.

One dollar can end up being less than 25 cents to your heirs.

> » *When Anthony's father passed away, he discovered that he was the beneficiary of his father's $500,000 IRA. Anthony*

has a wife and a family of four children, and he knew that his father had intended for a large portion of the IRA to go toward funding their college educations.

After Anthony's father's estate is distributed, Anthony, who is 50 years old and whose two oldest sons are entering college, liquidates the IRA. By doing so, his taxable income for that year puts him in a 39.6 percent tax bracket, immediately reducing the value of the asset to $302,000. An additional 3.8 percent surtax on net investment income further diminishes the funds to $283,000. Liquidating the IRA in effect subjects much of Anthony's regular income to the surtax, as well. At this point, Anthony will be taxed at 43.4 percent.

Anthony's state taxes are an additional 9 percent. Moreover, estate taxes on Anthony's father's assets claim another 22 percent. By the time the IRS is through, Anthony's income from the IRA will be taxed at 75 percent, leaving him with $125,000 of the original $500,000. While it would help contribute to the education of his children, it wouldn't come anywhere near completely paying for it, something the $500,000 could have easily done.

As the above example makes clear, leaving an asset to your beneficiaries can be more complicated than it may seem. In the case of a traditional IRA, after federal, estate and state taxes, the asset could literally diminish to as little as 25 percent of its value.

How does working with a professional help you make smarter tax decisions with your own finances? Any financial professional worth their salt will be working with a firm that has a team of trained tax professionals, including CPAs, who have an intimate knowledge of the tax code and how to adapt a financial plan to it.

BUILDING A TAX DIVERSIFIED PORTFOLIO

So far so good: avoid taxes, maximize your net annual income and have a plan for doing it. When people decide to leverage the experience and resources of a financial professional, they may not be thinking of how distribution planning and tax planning will benefit their portfolios. Often more exciting prospects like planning income annuities, investing in the market and structuring investments for growth rule the day. Taxes, however, play a crucial role in retirement planning. Achieving those tax goals requires knowledge of options, foresight and professional guidance.

Finding the path to a good tax plan isn't always a simple task. Every tax return you file is different from the one before it because things constantly change. Your expenses change. Planned or unplanned purchases occur. Health care costs, medical bills, an inheritance, property purchases, reaching an age where your RMD kicks in or travel, any number of things can affect how much income you report and how many deductions you take each year.

Preparing for the ever-changing landscape of your financial life requires a tax-diversified portfolio that can be leveraged to balance the incomes, expenditures and deductions that affect you each year. A financial professional will work with you to answer questions like these:

- What does your tax landscape look like?
- Do you have a tax-diversified portfolio robust enough to adapt to your needs?
- Do you have a diversity of taxable and non-taxable income planned for your retirement?
- Will you be able to maximize your distributions to take advantage of your deductions when you retire?
- Is your portfolio strong enough and tax-diversified enough to adapt to an ever-changing (and usually increasing) tax code?

» *When Rae returns home after a week in the hospital recovering from a knee replacement, the 77-year-old calls her daughter, sister and brother to let them know she is home and feeling well. She also should have called her CPA. Rae's medical expenses for the procedure, her hospital stay, her medications and the ongoing physical therapy she attended amount to more than $50,000.*

Currently, Americans can deduct medical expenses that are more than 7.5 percent of their Adjusted Gross Income (AGI). Rae's AGI is $60,000 the year of her knee replacement, meaning she is able to deduct $44,000 of her medical bills from her taxes that year. Her AGI dictated that she could deduct more than 80 percent of her medical expenses that year.

Rae didn't know this.

Had she been working with a financial professional who regularly asked her about any changes in her life, her spending, or her expenses (expected or unexpected), Rae could have saved thousands of dollars. The good news is that Rae can file an amendment to her tax return to recoup the overpayment.

This relatively simple example of how tax planning can save you money is just the tip of the iceberg. No one can be expected to know the entire U.S. tax code. But a professional who is working with a team of CPAs and financial professionals have an advantage over the average taxpayer who must start from square one on their own every year. Have you been taking advantage of all the deductions that are available to you?

ORANGE MONEY AND TAXES

There are also tax implications for the money that you have managed professionally. People with portions of their investment portfolio that are actively traded can particularly benefit from having a proactive tax strategy. Without going into too much detail, for tax purposes there are two kinds of investment money: qualified and non-qualified. Different investment strategies can have different effects on how you are taxed on your investments and the growth of your investments. Some are more beneficial for one kind of investment strategy over another. Determining how to plan for the taxation of non-qualified and qualified investments is fodder for holiday party discussions at accounting firms. While it may not be a stimulating topic for the average investor, you don't have to understand exactly how it works in order to benefit from it.

While there are many differences between qualified and non-qualified investments, the main difference is this: qualified plans are designed to give investors tax benefits by deferring taxation of their growth until they are withdrawn. Non-qualified investments are not eligible for these deferral benefits. As such, non-qualified investments are taxed whenever income is realized from them in the form of growth.

Actively and non-actively traded investments provide a simple example of how to position your investments for the best tax advantage. In an actively traded and managed portfolio, there is a high amount of buying and selling of stocks, bonds, funds, ETFs, etc. If that active portfolio of non-qualified investments does well and makes a 20 percent return one year and you are in the 39.6 percent tax bracket, your net gain from that portfolio is only about 12 percent (39.6 percent tax of the 20 percent gain is roughly 8 percent.) In a passive trading strategy, you can use a qualified investment tool, such as an IRA, to achieve 13, 14 or 15 percent growth (much lower than the actively traded portfolio), but still realize a higher net return because the growth of the qualified investment is not taxed until it is withdrawn.

Does this mean that you have to always rely on a buy and hold strategy in qualified investment tools? Not necessarily. The question is, if you have qualified and non-qualified investments, where do you want to position your actively traded and managed assets? Incorporating a planful approach to positioning your investments for more beneficial taxation can be done many ways, but let's consider one example. Keeping your actively managed investment strategies inside an IRA or some other qualified plan could allow you to realize the higher gains of those investments without paying tax on their growth every year. Your more passively managed funds could then be kept in taxable, non-qualified vehicles and methods, and because you aren't realizing income from them on an annual basis by frequently trading them, they grow sheltered from taxation.

If you are interested in taking advantage of tax strategies that maximize your net income, you need the attentive strategies, experience and knowledge of a professional who can give you options that position you for profit. At the end of the day, what's important to you as the consumer is how much you keep, your after-tax take home.

ESTATE TAXES

The government doesn't just tax your income from investments while you're alive. They will also dip into your legacy.

While estate taxes aren't as hot of a topic as they were a few years ago, they are still an issue of concern for many people with assets. While taxes may not apply on estates that are less than $5 million, certain states have estate taxes with much lower exclusion ratios. Some are as low as $600,000. Many people may have to pay a state estate tax. One strategy for avoiding those types of taxes is to move assets outside of your estate. That can include gifting them to family or friends, or putting them into an irrevocable trust. Life insurance is another option for protecting your legacy.

CHAPTER 9 RECAP //

- When you report your taxes, you are paying to record history. When you *plan* your taxes with a financial professional, you are proactively finding the best options for your tax return. Planning proactively means more money in your wallet and less money into the hands of Uncle Sam.

- It's important to understand the tax repercussions when tapping into assets from a 401(k) or a traditional IRA for use as an income source. Money that is considered qualified by the Federal government must be taxed upon distribution. Any gains made on annuities will be taxed if the annuity was purchased with non-qualified money.

- At the age of 70 ½, the Federal Government requires all IRA participants to take their RMD, or Required Minimum Distribution. Failure to take your RMD can cost you thousands of dollars in taxes and penalty fees.

- Taxes play an important role during your retirement. It's important that you understand your obligations, and the differences between tax-deferred and tax-advantaged accounts.

- You make more money by saving on taxes than you do by making more money. This simple concept becomes extremely valuable to people in retirement and those living on fixed incomes.

10

Tax Evasion Vs Tax Avoidance: Choose Wisely

When will my taxes go up?

Louis Brandeis provides one of the best examples illustrating how tax planning works. Brandeis was Associate Justice on the Supreme Court of the United States from 1916 to 1939. Born in Louisville, Kentucky, Brandeis was an intelligent man with a touch of country charm. He described tax planning this way:

"I live in Alexandria, Virginia. Near the Court Chambers, there is a toll bridge across the Potomac. When in a rush, I pay the dollar toll and get home early. However, I usually drive outside the downtown section of the city and cross the Potomac on a free bridge.

The bridge was placed outside the downtown Washington, D.C. area to serve a useful social service—getting drivers to drive the extra mile and help alleviate congestion during the rush hour.

If I went over the toll bridge and through the barrier without paying a toll, I would be committing tax evasion.

If I drive the extra mile and drive outside the city of Washington to the free bridge, I am using a legitimate, logical and suitable method of tax avoidance, and I am performing a useful social service by doing so.

*The tragedy is that **few people know that the free bridge exists.**"*

Like Brandeis, most American taxpayers have options when it comes to "crossing the Potomac," so to speak. It's a financial planner's job to tell you what options are available. You can wait until March to file your taxes, at which time you might pay someone to report and pay the government a larger portion of your income. However, you could instead begin preparations before the end of the year, work with your financial professional and incorporate a tax plan as part of your overall financial planning strategy. Filing later is like crossing the toll bridge. Tax planning is like crossing the free bridge.

Which would you rather do?

The answer to this question is easy. Most people want to save money and pay less in taxes. What makes this situation really difficult in real life however is that the signs along the side of the road that direct us to the free bridge are not that clear. To normal Americans, and to plenty of people who have studied it, the U.S. tax code is easy to get lost in. There are all kinds of rules, exceptions to rules, caveats and conditions that are difficult to understand, or even to know about. What you really need to know are your options and the bottom line impacts of those options.

ROTH IRA CONVERSIONS

The attractive qualities of Roth IRAs may have prompted you to explore the possibility of moving some of your assets into a Roth account. Another important difference between the accounts is how they treat Required Minimum Distributions (RMDs). When you turn 70 ½ years old, you are required to take a minimum amount of money out of a traditional IRA. This amount is your RMD. It is treated as taxable income. Roth IRAs, however, do not have RMDs, and their distributions are not taxable. Quite a deal, right?

While having a Roth IRA as part of your portfolio is a good idea, converting assets to a Roth IRA can pose some challenges, depending on what kinds of assets you want to transfer.

One common option is the conversion of a traditional IRA to a Roth IRA. You may have heard about converting your IRA to a Roth IRA, but you might not know the full net result on your income. The main difference between the two accounts is that the growth of investments within a traditional IRA is not taxed until income is withdrawn from the account, whereas taxes are charged on contribution amounts to a Roth IRA, not withdrawals. The problem, however, is that when assets are removed from a traditional IRA, even if the assets are being transferred to a Roth IRA account, taxes apply.

There are a lot of reasons to look at Roth conversions. People have a lot of money in IRAs, up to multiple millions of dollars. Even with $500,000, when they turn 70 ½ years old, their RMD is going to be approximately $18,000, and they have to take that out whether they want to or not. It's a tax issue. Essentially, if you will be subject to high RMDs, it could have impacts on how much of your Social Security is taxable, and on your tax bracket.

By paying taxes now instead of later on assets in a Roth IRA, you can realize tax-advantaged growth. You pay once and you're done paying. Your heirs are done paying. It's a powerful tool. Here's a simple example to show you how powerful it can be:

Imagine that you pay to convert a traditional IRA to a Roth. You have decided that you want to put the money in a vehicle that gives you a tax-advantaged income option down the road. If you pay a 25 percent tax on that conversion and the Roth IRA then doubles in value over the next 10 years, you could look at your situation as only having paid 12.5 percent tax.

The prospect of tax-advantaged income is a tempting one. While you have to pay a conversion tax to transfer your assets, you also have turned taxable income into tax free retirement money that you can let grow as long as you want without being required to withdraw it.

There are options, however, that address this problem. Much like the Brandeis story, there may be a "free bridge" option for many investors.

Your financial professional will likely tell you that it is not a matter of whether or not you should perform a Roth IRA conversion, it is a matter of how much you should convert and when.

Here are some of the things to consider before converting to a Roth IRA:

- If you make a conversion before you retire, you may end up paying higher taxes on the conversion because it is likely that you are in some of your highest earning years, placing you in the highest tax bracket of your life. It is possible that a better strategy would be to wait until after you retire, a time when you may have less taxable income, which would place you in a lower tax bracket.

- Many people opt to reduce their work hours from fulltime to part-time in the years before they retire. If you have pursued this option, your income will likely be lower, in turn lowering your tax rate.

- The first years that you draw Social Security benefits can also be years of lower reported income, making it another good time frame in which to convert to a Roth IRA.

One key strategy to handling a Roth IRA conversion is to ***always be able to pay the cost of the conversion tax with outside money***. Structuring your tax year to include something like a significant deduction can help you offset the conversion tax. This way you aren't forced to take the money you need for taxes from the value of the IRA. The reason taxes apply to this maneuver is because when you withdraw money from a traditional IRA, it is treated as taxable income by the IRS. Your financial professional, with the help of the CPAs at their firm, may be able to provide you with options like after-tax money, itemized deductions or other situations that can pose effective tax avoidance options.

Some examples of avoiding Roth IRA conversions taxes include:

- *Using medical expenses that are above 10 percent of your Adjusted Gross Income.* If you have health care costs that you can list as itemized deductions, you can convert an amount of income from a traditional IRA to a Roth IRA that is offset by the deductible amount. Essentially, deductible medical expenses negate the taxes resulting from recording the conversion.
- *Individuals, usually small business owners, who are dealing with a Net Operating Loss (NOL).* If you have NOLs, but aren't able to utilize all of them on your tax return, you can carry them forward to offset the taxable income from the taxes on income you convert to a Roth IRA.
- *Charitable giving.* If you are charitably inclined, you can use the amount of your donations to reduce the amount of taxable income you have during that year. By matching the amount you convert to a Roth IRA to the amount

your taxable income was reduced by charitable giving, you can essentially avoid taxation on the conversion. You may decide to double your donations to a charity in one year, giving them two years' worth of donations in order to offset the Roth IRA conversion tax on this year's tax return.

- *Investments that are subject to depletion.* Certain investments can kick off depletion expenses. If you make an investment and are subject to depletion expenses, they can be deducted and used to offset a Roth IRA conversion tax.

Not all of the above scenarios work for everyone, and there are many other options for offsetting conversion taxes. The point is that you have options, and your financial professional and tax professional can help you understand those options.

If you have a traditional IRA, Roth conversions are something you should look at. As you approach retirement you should consider your options and make choices that keep more of your money in your pocket, not the government's.

ADDITIONAL TAX BENEFITS OF ROTH IRAS

Not only do Roth IRAs provide you with tax-advantaged growth, they also give you a tax diversified landscape that allows you to maximize your distributions. Chances are that no matter the circumstances, you will have taxed income and other assets subject to taxation. ***But if you have a Roth IRA, you have the unique ability to manage your Adjusted Gross Income (AGI), because you have a tax-advantaged income option!***

Converting to a Roth IRA can also help you preserve and build your legacy. Because Roth IRAs are exempt from RMDs, after you make a conversion from a traditional IRA, your Roth account can grow tax-advantaged for another 15, 20 or 25 years and it can be used as tax-advantaged income by your heirs. It is important to note, however, that non-spousal beneficiaries do have to take RMDs from a Roth IRA, or choose to stretch it and draw tax-advantaged income out of it over their lifetime.

TO CONVERT OR NOT TO CONVERT?

Conversions aren't only for retirees. You can convert at any time. Your choice should be based on your individual circumstances and tax situation. Sticking with a traditional IRA or converting to a Roth, again, depends on your individual circumstances, including your income, your tax bracket and the amount of deductions you have each year.

Is it better to have a Roth IRA or traditional IRA? It depends on your individual circumstance. Some people don't mind having taxable income from an IRA. Their income might not be very high and their RMD might not bump their tax bracket up, so it's not as big a deal. A similar situation might involve income from Social Security. Social Security benefits are taxed based on other income you are drawing. If you are in a position where none or very little of your Social Security benefit is subject to taxes, paying income tax on your RMD may be very easy.

> » *There are also situations where leveraging taxable income from a traditional IRA can work to your advantage come tax time. For example, Darrel and Linda dream of buying a boat when they retire. It is something they have looked forward to their entire marriage. In addition to the savings and investments that they created to supply them with income during retirement, which includes a traditional IRA, they have also saved money for the sole purpose of purchasing a boat once they stop working.*
>
> *When the time comes and they finally buy the boat of their dreams, they pay an additional $15,000 in sales taxes that year because of the large purchase. Because they are retired*

and earning less money, the deductions they used to be able to realize from their income taxes are no longer there. The high amount of sales taxes they paid on the boat puts them in a position where they could benefit from taking taxable income from a traditional IRA.

When Darrel and Linda's financial professional learns about their purchase, he immediately contacts a CPA at his firm to run the numbers. They determine that by taking a $15,000 distribution from their IRA, they could fulfill their income needs to offset the $15,000 sales tax deduction that they were claiming due to the purchase of their boat. In the end, they pay zero taxes on their income distribution from their IRA.

The moral of the story? **Having a tax diversified landscape gives you options.** Having capital assets that can be liquidated, tax-advantaged income options and sources that can create capital gains or capital losses will put you in a position to play your cards right no matter what you want to accomplish with your taxes. The ace up your sleeve is your financial professional and the CPAs they work with. Do yourself a favor and *plan* your taxes instead of *reporting* them!

WHAT TO DO ABOUT RISING TAXES

If you were one of the people who raised your hand in response to the question, "How many people think taxes will go up?" a brief look at American history will further prove you right.

How do you prepare? Now is the time to take action and structure countermeasures for the good, the bad and the ugly of each of these legislative nightmares through tax-advantaged retirement planning.

You make more money by saving on taxes than you do by making more money. The simplistic logic of the statement makes sense when you discover it takes $1.50 in earnings to put that same dollar, saved in taxes, back in your pocket.

As simple as it sounds, it is much more difficult to execute. Most people fail to put together a plan as they near retirement, beginning with a simple cash flow budget. If you have not analyzed your proposed income streams and expenses, you could not possibly have taken the time to position these cash flows and other events into a tax-preferred plan.

Most people will state that they have a plan and, thus, do not need any further assistance in this area. The truth in most instances is that people could not show you their plan, and among the few that could, most would not be able to show you how they have executed it. In this regard, they might as well be Richard Nixon stating, "I am not a crook" for as much as they state, "I have a plan." The truth lies in waiting. As we approach or begin retirement, we should look at what cash flows we will have. Do we have a pension? How about Social Security? How much additional cash flow am I going to need to draw from my assets to maintain the lifestyle that I desire?

We spend our whole lives saving and accumulating wealth but spend so little time determining how to distribute this accumulation so as to retain it. We need to make sure we have the appropriate diversification of taxable versus non-taxable assets to complement our distribution strategy.

THE BENEFITS OF DIVERSIFICATION

Heading into retirement, we should be situated with a diversified tax landscape. The point to spending our whole lives accumulating wealth is not to see the size of the number on paper, but rather to be an exercise in how much we put in our pocket after removing it from the paper. To truly understand tax diversification, we must understand what types of money exist and how each of these will be treated during accumulation and, most importantly, during distribution. The following is a brief summary:

1. Free Money
2. Tax-advantaged money
3. Tax-deferred money
4. Taxable money
   a. Ordinary income
   b. Capital gains and qualified dividends

FREE MONEY

Free money is the best kind of money regardless of tax treatment because, in the end, you have more money than you would have otherwise. Many employers will provide contributions toward employee retirement accounts to offer additional employment benefits and encourage employees to save for their own retirement. With this, employers often will offer a matching contribution in which they contribute up to a certain percentage of an employee's salary (generally three to five percent) toward that employee's retirement account when the employee contributes to their retirement account as well. For example, if an employee earns $50,000 annually and contributes three percent ($1,500) to their retirement account annually, the employer will also contribute three percent ($1,500) to the employee's account. That is $1,500 in free money. Take all you can get! Bear in mind that any employer contribution to a 401(k) will still be subject to taxation when withdrawn.

TAX-ADVANTAGED MONEY

Tax-advantaged money is the next best thing to free money. Although you have to earn tax-advantaged money, you do not have to give part of it away to Uncle Sam. Tax-advantaged money comes in three basic forms that you can utilize during your lifetime (four if prison inspires your future, but we are not going to discuss that option!).

One of the most commonly known forms of tax-advantaged money is municipal bonds, which earn and pay interest that could be tax-advantaged on the federal level, state level, or both. There are several caveats that should be discussed with regard to the notion of tax-advantaged income from municipal bonds. First, you will notice that tax-advantaged has several flavors from the state and federal perspective. This is because states will generally tax the interest earned on a municipal bond unless the bond is offered from an entity located within that state. This severely limits the availability of completely tax-advantaged municipal bonds and constrains underlying risk and liquidity factors. Second, municipal bond interest is added back into the equation for determining your modified adjusted gross income (MAGI) for Social Security. This could push your income above a threshold and subject a portion of your Social Security income to taxation.

In effect, if this interest subjects some other income to taxation then this interest is truly being taxed.

Last, municipal bond interest may be excluded from the regular federal tax system, but it is included for determining tax under the alternative minimum tax (AMT) system. In its basic form, the AMT system is a separate tax system that applies if the tax computed under AMT exceeds the tax computed under the regular tax system. The difference between these two computations is the alternative minimum tax.

TAX-ADVANTAGED MONEY: ROTH IRA

Roth accounts are probably the single greatest tax asset that has come from Congress outside of life insurance. They are well known but rarely used. Roth IRAs were first established by the Taxpayer Relief Act of 1997 and named after Senator William Roth, the chief sponsor of the legislation. Roth accounts are simply an account in the form of an individual retirement account or an employer sponsored retirement account that allows for tax-advantaged growth of earnings and, thus, tax-advantaged income.

The main difference between a Roth and a traditional IRA or employer-sponsored plan lies in the timing of the taxation. We are all very familiar with the typical scenario of putting money away for retirement through an employer plan, whereby they deduct money from our paychecks and put it directly into a retirement account. This money is taken out before taxes are calculated, meaning we do not pay tax on those earnings today. A Roth account, on the other hand, takes the money after the taxes have been removed and puts it into the retirement account, so we do pay tax on the money today. The other significant difference between these two is taxation during distribution in later years. Regarding our traditional retirement accounts, when we take the money out later it is added to our ordinary income and is taxed accordingly. Additionally, including this in our income subjects us to the consequences mentioned above for municipal bonds with Social Security taxation, AMT, as well as higher Medicare premiums. A Roth on the other hand is distributed tax-advantaged and does not contribute toward negative impact items such as Social Security taxation, AMT, or Medicare premium increases. It essentially comes back to us without tax and other obligations.

The best way to view the difference between the two accounts is to look at the life of a farmer. A farmer will buy seed, plant it in the ground, grow the crops and harvest it later for sale. Typically, the farmer would only pay tax on the crops that have been harvested and sold. But if you were the farmer, would you rather pay tax on the $5,000 of seed that you plant today or the $50,000 of crops harvested later? The obvious answer is $5,000 of seed today. The truth to the matter is that you are a farmer, except you plant dollars into your retirement account instead of seeds into the earth.

So why doesn't everyone have a Roth retirement account if things are so simple? There are several reasons, but the single greatest reason has been the constraints on contributions. If you earned over certain thresholds (MAGI over $125,000 single and $183,000 joint for 2012), you were not eligible to make contributions, and until last year, if your modified adjusted gross income (MAGI) was over $100,000 (single or joint), you could not convert a traditional IRA to a Roth. Outside these contribution limits, most people save for retirement through their employers and most employers still do not offer Roth options in their plans. The reason behind this is because Roth accounts are not that well understood and people have been educated to believe that saving on taxes today is the best possible course of action.

TAX-ADVANTAGED MONEY: LIFE INSURANCE

As previously mentioned, the single greatest tax asset that has come from Congress outside of life insurance is the Roth account. Life insurance is the little-known or little-discussed tax asset that holds some of the greatest value in your financial history both during life and upon death. It is by far the best tax-advantaged device available. We traditionally view life insurance as a way to protect our loved ones from financial ruin upon our demise and it should be noted that everyone who cares about someone should have life insurance. Purchasing a life insurance policy ensures that our loved ones will receive income from the life insurance company to help them pay our final expenses and carry on with their lives without us comfortably when we die. The best part of the life insurance windfall is the fact that nobody will have to pay tax on the money received. This is the single greatest tax-advantaged device available, but it has one downside, we do not get to use it. Only our heirs will.

The little known and even less discussed part of life insurance is the cash value build-up within whole life and universal life (permanent) policies. Life insurance is not typically seen as an investment vehicle for building wealth and retirement planning, although we should discuss briefly why this thought process should be re-evaluated. Permanent life insurance is generally misconceived as something that is very expensive for a wealth accumulation vehicle because there are mortality charges (fees for the death benefit) that detract from the available returns. Furthermore, those returns do not yield as much as the stock market over the long run. This is why many times you will hear the phrase "buy term and invest the rest," where "term" refers to term insurance.

Let us take a second to review two terms just used in regard to life insurance: term and permanent. Term insurance is an idea with which most people are familiar. You purchase a certain death benefit that will go to your heirs upon death and this policy will be in effect for a certain number of years, typically 10 to 20 years. The 10 to 20 years is the term of the policy and once you have reached that end you no longer have insurance unless you purchase another policy, or pay a significantly increased premium.

Permanent insurance on the other hand has no term involved. It is permanent as long as the premiums continue to be paid. Generally speaking, permanent insurance initially has higher premiums than term insurance for the same amount of death benefit coverage and it is this difference that is referred to when people say "invest the rest."

Simply speaking there are significant differences between these two policies that are not often considered when providing a comparative analysis of the numbers. One item that gets lost in the fray when comparing term and permanent insurance is that term usually expires before death. In fact, insurance studies show less than one percent of all term policies pay out death benefit claims. The issue arises when the term expires and the desire to have more insurance is still present.

A term policy with the same benefit will be much more expensive than the original policy and, many times, life events occur, such as cancer or heart conditions, which makes it impossible to acquire another policy and leaves your loved ones unprotected and tax-advantaged legacy planning out of the equation.

Another aspect and probably the most important piece in consideration of the future of taxation is the fact that permanent insurance has a cash accumulation value. Two aspects stand out with the cash accumulation value. First, as the cash accumulation value increases the death benefit will also increase whereas term insurance remains level. Second, if structured properly, this cash accumulation offers value to you during your lifetime rather than to your heirs upon death. The cash accumulation value can be used for tax-advantaged income during your lifetime through policy loans. Most importantly, this tax-advantaged income is available during retirement for distribution planning, all while offering the same typical financial protection to your heirs.

TAX-DEFERRED MONEY

Tax-deferred money is the type of money with which most of people are familiar, but we also briefly reviewed the idea above. Tax-deferred money is typically our traditional IRA, employer sponsored retirement plan or a non-qualified annuity. Essentially, you put money into an investment vehicle that will accumulate in value over time and you do not pay taxes on the earnings that grow these accounts until you distribute them. Once the money is distributed, taxes must be paid. However, the same negative consequences exist with regard to additional taxation and expense in other areas as previously discussed.

TAXABLE MONEY

Taxable money is everything else and is taxable today, later or whenever it is received. These four types of money come down to two distinct classifications: taxable and tax-free. The greatest difference when comparing taxable and tax-advantaged income is a function of how much money we keep after tax. For help in determining what the differences should be, excluding outside factors such as Social Security taxation and AMT, a tax equivalent yield should be used.

TAX-ADVANTAGED IN THE REAL WORLD

To put the tax equivalent yield into perspective, let us look at an example: Bob and Mary are currently retired, living on Social Security and interest from investments and falling within the 25 percent tax bracket. They have a substantial portion of their investments in municipal bonds yielding 6 percent, which is quite comforting in today's market. The tax equivalent yield they would need to earn from a taxable investment would be 8 percent, a 2 percent gap that seems almost impossible given current market volatility. However, something that has never been put into perspective is that the interest from their municipal bonds is subject to taxation on their Social Security benefits (at 21.25 percent). With this, the yield on their municipal bonds would be 4.725 percent, and the taxable equivalent yield falls to 6.3 percent, leaving a gap of only 1.575 percent.

In the end, most people spend their lives accumulating wealth through the best, if not the only vehicle they know, a tax-deferred account. This account is most likely a 401(k) or 403(b) plan offered through their employer and may be supplemented with an IRA that was established at one point or another. As the years go by, people blindly throw money into these accounts in an effort to save for a retirement that we someday hope to reach.

The truth is, most people have an age selected for when they would like to retire, but spend their lives wondering if they will ever be able to actually quit working. To answer this question, you must understand how much money you will have available to contribute toward your needs. *In other words, you need to know what your after-tax income will be during this period.*

All else being equal, it would not matter if you put your money into a taxable, tax-deferred or tax-advantaged account as long as income tax rates never change and outside factors are never an event. The net amount you receive in the end will be the same.

Unfortunately, this will never be the case. We believe most adamantly that taxes will increase in the future, meaning we will likely see higher taxes in retirement than during our peak earning years.

Regardless, saving for retirement in any form is a good thing as it appears from all practical perspectives that future government benefits will be cut and taxes will increase. You have the ability to plan today for efficient tax diversification and maximization of your after-tax dollars during your distribution years.

CHAPTER 10 RECAP //

- Look for the "free bridge" option in your tax strategy.
- Converting from a traditional to a Roth IRA can provide you with tax-advantaged retirement income and help you preserve and build your legacy.
- Most people are familiar with tax-deferred methods of retirement savings such a traditional IRAs. By taking action now, you can prepare for the rise in taxes by restructuring your assets to include the benefits of free and tax-advantaged money.
- Tax-advantaged money is money you earn without having to pay taxes on. One of the most common forms includes municipal bonds, but be aware these come with many state and federal caveats and complexities.
- Roth IRAs and Life Insurance are two forms of tax-advantaged money that can take advantage of today's lower tax rate when preparing for tomorrow's retirement.

11

Building a Legacy or Just Creating Documents?

Will my family be taken care of?

Dee Booth lived in Georgia and was diagnosed with a terminal illness. The doctor only gave her three or four months to live. Dee wanted to make sure her family was taken care of, and so together with her husband, George, they set about preparing. They went to a local attorney to prepare all of their documents. They had an estate worth $1 million and $300,000 of that estate was in her name. Most of the investment assets were in his name. Dee had real estate, including property out-of-state which she had inherited together with two of her sisters. She and her sisters also had land in South Georgia that they owned jointly. Dee's wishes were to make sure that the home she and George lived in went to her husband. She wanted her share of the land investments and a retirement account valued at $120,000 *to go to their children. Everything else she wanted to go directly to her husband, George, via her Will.*

George and Dee signed all the documents. A few weeks later, Dee was having trouble sleeping. She was worried about the house and wanted to make absolutely sure that her husband would receive their home at her death. Together they went back to the attorney and the attorney did a quitclaim deed to her husband. That set Dee's mind at ease, since the house was now totally in her husband's name. Six weeks later, she passed away.

To get help with the settlement of his wife's estate, George went to see a financial professional who had a team of experts educated in estate planning. What they saw really made them heartsick because almost nothing that Dee had wanted to happen actually happened. Dee had created documents, but she had not created a strategy and plan.

The problem with a lot of legacy planning done today is that there is no coaching, no guidance and no actual estate planning. When most people think about an estate, it may seem like something only the very wealthy have: a stately manor or an enormous business. But everybody has something they want to pass down, regardless of how much or how little.

In the case of Dee Booth, she wanted the land she owned jointly with her sisters to be passed on to her children. It did not go to her children because it was titled "joint tenants with rights of survivorship" which means the land automatically went to the other two sisters. The land she had in South Georgia didn't go to the children because once again, it was titled incorrectly and so it went to the husband. The retirement account valued at $120,000 also went to the husband because he was listed as the beneficiary. It didn't go through the Will at all because **beneficiary forms takes precedent over wills, trusts, and divorce decrees.** Once again, the children did not get what they were supposed to get.

To make matters even worse, 18 months later George remarried his late wife's acquaintance who happened to be someone Dee really didn't like. Dee did not get along with this lady when she was living but now, guess who has control of her $120,000 and the land that was supposed to go to her children? George's new wife.

Today, there is more to consider when planning a legacy other than just what you want to leave behind. You want to ensure that the right people get what you intended while also taking the time to explore strategies that can maximize the financial benefit to the ones you care about. George and Dee Booth took the time to have someone create the documents, but they didn't design a plan as a whole and coordinate all of their assets and accounts. All of their deeds and accounts did not hold the correct beneficiaries and this created a heartbreaking problem because Dee's children did not get the inheritance that she had intended.

COORDINATING THE PAPERWORK

The distribution of your assets, whether in the form of property, stocks, Individual Retirement Accounts, 401(k)s or liquid assets, can be a complicated undertaking if you haven't left clear instructions about how you want them handled. Not having a plan will cost more money and take more time, leaving your loved ones to wait (sometimes for years) and receive less of your legacy than if you had a clear plan.

Life is short, and the relatively complicated nature of sorting through your assets can feel like a daunting task. But one thing is for sure: *it is impossible for your assets to be transferred or distributed the way you want at the end of your life if you don't have a plan.*

Ask yourself:

- Are my assets up to date?

- Have my primary and contingent beneficiaries been clearly designated? Updated?
- Does my plan allow for restriction of a beneficiary?
- Does my legacy plan address minor children that I want to provide with income?
- Does my legacy plan allow for multi-generational payout?

Answers to these questions are critical if you want the final say in how your assets are distributed. In order to achieve your legacy goals, you need a plan.

Eventually, when your income need is filled and you have sufficient standby money to meet your need for emergencies, travel or other extra expenses you are planning for, whatever isn't used during your lifetime becomes your financial legacy. The money that you do not use during your lifetime will either go to loved ones, charities, attorneys, or the IRS. The questions is, who would you rather disinherit?

By having a legacy plan that clearly outlines your assets, your beneficiaries and your distribution goals, you can make sure that your money and property is ending up in the hands of the people you determine beforehand. Is it really that big of a deal? It absolutely is! Think about it. Without a clear plan, it is impossible for anyone to know if your beneficiary designations are current and reflect your wishes because you haven't clearly expressed who your beneficiaries are. You may have an idea of who you want your assets to go to, but without a plan, it is anyone's guess. It is also impossible to know if the titling of your assets is accurate unless you have gone through and determined whose name is on the titles. More importantly, *if you have not clearly and effectively communicated your desires regarding the planned distribution of your legacy, you and your family may end up losing a large part of it.*

As you can see, managing a legacy is more complicated than having an attorney read your will, divide your estate and write checks to your heirs. The additional issue of taxes, Family Maximum Benefit calculations and a host of other decisions rear their heads. Educating yourself about the best options for positioning your legacy assets is a challenging undertaking. Working with a financial professional who is versed in determining the most efficient and effective ways of preserving and distributing your legacy can save you time, money and strife.

So, how do you begin?

Making a Legacy Plan Starts with a Simple List. The first, and one of the largest, steps to setting up an estate plan with a financial professional that reflects your desires is creating a detailed inventory of your assets and debts (if you have any). You need to know what assets you have, who the beneficiaries are, how much they are worth and how they are titled. You can start by identifying and listing your assets. This is a good starting point for working with a financial professional who can then help you determine the detailed information about your assets that will dictate how they are distributed upon your death.

If you are particularly concerned about leaving your kids and grandkids a lifetime of income with minimal taxes, you will want to discuss a Stretch IRA option with your financial professional.

STRETCH IRAS: GETTING THE MOST OUT OF YOUR MONEY

In 1986, the U.S. Congress passed a law that allows for multi-generational distributions of IRA assets. This type of distribution is called a Stretch IRA because it stretches the distribution of the account out over a longer period of time to several beneficiaries. It also allows the account to continue accumulating value throughout your relatives' lifetimes. You can use a Stretch IRA as an income tool that distributes throughout your lifetime, your children's lifetimes and your grandchildren's lifetimes.

Stretch IRAs are an attractive option for those more concerned with creating income for their loved ones than leaving them with a lump sum that may be subject to a high tax rate. With traditional IRA distributions, non-spousal beneficiaries must generally take distributions from their inherited IRAs, whether transferred or not, within five years after the death of the IRA owner. An exception to this rule applies if the beneficiary elects to take distributions over his or her lifetime, which is referred to as stretching the IRA.

Let's begin by looking at the potential of stretching an IRA throughout multiple generations.

> » In this scenario, Mr. Cleaver has an IRA with a current balance of $350,000. If we assume a five percent annual rate of return, and a 28 percent tax rate, the Stretch IRA turned a $502,625 legacy into more than $1.5 million. Doubling the value of the IRA also provided Mr. Cleaver, his wife, two children and three grandchildren with income. Not choosing the stretch option would have cost nearly $800,000 and had impacts on six of Mr. Cleaver's loved ones.

Unfortunately, many things may also play a role in failing to stretch IRA distributions. It can be tempting for a beneficiary to take a lump sum of money despite the tax consequences. Fortunately, if you want to solidify your plan for distribution, there are options that will allow you to open up an IRA and incorporate "spendthrift" clauses for your beneficiaries. This will ensure your legacy is stretched appropriately and to your specifications. Only certain insurance companies allow this option, and you will not find this benefit with any brokerage accounts. You need to work

Beneficiaries Stretch IRA Distributions

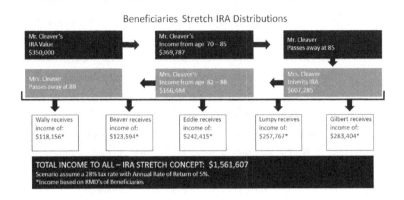

TOTAL INCOME TO ALL – IRA STRETCH CONCEPT: $1,561,607
Scenario assume a 28% tax rate with Annual Rate of Return of 5%.
*Income based on RMD's of Beneficiaries

Beneficiaries FAIL to Stretch IRA Distributions

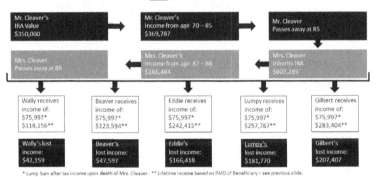

* Lump Sum after tax income upon death of Mrs. Cleaver.   ** Lifetime income based on RMD of Beneficiary – see previous slide.

with a financial professional who has the appropriate relationship with an insurance company that provides this option.

AVOIDING LEGACY MISTAKES
Unfortunately, even with the best of intentions, mistakes can easily happen when planning for what you want to leave behind. In the following story, the two main problems that arose for Thomas were *Probate* and *Unintentional Disinheritance:*

» *Thomas organized his assets long ago. He started planning his retirement early and made investment decisions that would meet his needs. With a combination of IRA to Roth IRA conversions, a series of income annuities and a well-planned money management strategy overseen by his financial professional, he easily filled his income gap and was able to focus on ways to accumulate his wealth throughout his retirement. He reorganized his Safe Side and Risk Side Money as he got older. When Thomas retired, he had an income plan created that allowed him to maximize his Social Security benefit. He even had enough to accumulate wealth during his retirement. At this point, Thomas turned his attention to planning his legacy. He wanted to know how he could maximize the amount of money he will pass on to his heirs.*

Thomas met with an attorney to draw up a will, but he quickly learned that while having a will was a good plan, it wasn't the most efficient way to distribute his legacy. In fact, relying solely on a will created several roadblocks.

Problem #1: Probate

Probate. Just speaking the word out loud can cause shivers to run down your spine. Probate's ugly reputation is well deserved. It can be a costly, time consuming process that diminishes your estate and can delay the distribution of your estate to your loved ones. Nasty stuff, by any measure. Unless you have made a clear legacy plan and discussed options for avoiding probate, it is highly likely that you have many assets that might pass through probate needlessly. ***If your will and beneficiary designations aren't correctly structured, some of these assets will go through the probate process, which can turn dollars into cents.***

If you have a will, probate is usually just a formality. There is little risk that your will won't be executed per your instructions. The problem arises when the costs and lengthy timeline that probate creates come into play. Probate proceedings are notoriously expensive, lengthy and ponderous. A typical probate process identifies all of your assets and debts, pays any taxes and fees that you owe (including estate tax), pays court fees, and distributes your property and assets to your heirs. This process usually takes at least a year, and can take even longer before your heirs actually receive anything that you have left for them. For this reason, and because of the sometimes exorbitant fees that may be charged by lawyers and accountants during the process, probate has earned a nasty reputation.

Probate can also be a painstakingly public process. Because the probate process happens in court, the assets you own that go through a probate procedure become part of the public record. While this may not seem like a big deal to some, other people don't want that kind of intimate information available to the public.

Additionally, if your estate is entirely distributed via your will, the money that your family may need to cover the costs of your medical bills, funeral expenses and estate taxes will be tied up in probate, which can last up to a year or more. While immediate family members may have the option of requesting immediate cash from your assets during probate to cover immediate health care expenses, taxes, and fees, that process comes with its own set of complications. Choosing alternative methods for distributing your legacy can make life easier for your loved ones and can help them claim more of your estate in a more timely fashion than traditional methods.

A simpler and less tedious approach is to avoid probate altogether by structuring your estate to be distributed outside of the probate process. Two common ways of doing this are by structuring your assets inside a life insurance plan, and by using individual retirement planning tools like IRAs that give you the option of designating a beneficiary upon your death.

» *Andy and his wife, Katie, were in their late 60s. Katie worked for 35 years as a nurse and when she passed away, she left her husband with about $1 million in assets. It was Katie's intention that their two children, Luke and Katelyn, receive some of this money.*

One year later, Andy remarried. He bought a new house and listed his new wife as the beneficiary. Five years later, when Andy passed away, his new wife inherited all his assets. Andy unintentionally disinherited his children from his previous marriage. Everything his first wife, Katie, worked so hard for goes to his new wife and Luke and Katelyn receive nothing.

Problem #2: Unintentionally Disinheriting Your Family

You would never want to unintentionally disinherit a loved one or loved ones because of confusion surrounding your legacy plan. Unfortunately, it happens. Why? This terrible situation is typically caused by a simple lack of understanding. In particular, mistakes regarding legacy distribution occur with regards to those whom people care for the most: their grandchildren.

One of the most important ways to plan for the inheritance of your grandchildren is by properly structuring the distribution of your legacy. Specifically, you need to know if your legacy is going to be distributed *per stirpes* or *per capita*.

Per Stirpes. *Per stirpes* is a legal term in Latin that means "by the branch." Your estate will be distributed *per stirpes* if you designate each branch of your family to receive an equal share of your estate. In the event that your children predecease you, their share will be distributed evenly between their children — your grandchildren.

Per Capita. *Per capita* distribution is different in that you may designate different amounts of your estate to be distributed to members of the same generation.

Per stirpes distribution of assets will follow the family tree down the line as the predecessor beneficiaries pass away. On the other hand, per capita distribution of assets ends on the branch of the family tree with the death of a designated beneficiary. For example, when your child passes away, in a per capita distribution, your grandchildren would not receive distributions from the assets that you designated to your child.

What the terms mean is not nearly as important as what they do, however. The reality is that improperly titled assets could accidentally leave your grandchildren disinherited upon the death of their parents. It's easy to check, and it's even easier to fix.

A simple way to remember the difference between the two types of distribution goes something like this: "***Stripes are forever and Capita is capped.***"

Another way to avoid complicated legacy distribution problems, and the probate process, is by leveraging a life insurance plan.

LIFE INSURANCE: AN IMPORTANT LEGACY TOOL

One of the most powerful legacy tools you can leverage is a good life insurance policy. Life insurance is a highly efficient legacy tool because it creates money when it is needed or desired the most. Over the years, life insurance has become less expensive, while it offers more features, and provides longer guarantees.

There are many unique benefits of life insurance that can help your beneficiaries get the most out of your legacy. Some of them include:

- Providing beneficiaries with a tax-free, liquid asset.
- Covering the costs associated with your death.
- Providing income for your dependents.
- Offering an investment opportunity for your beneficiaries.
- Covering expenses such as tuition or mortgage down payments for your children or grandchildren.

Very few people want life insurance, but nearly everyone wants what it does. Life insurance is specifically, and uniquely, capable of creating money when it is needed most. When a loved one passes, no amount of money can remove the pain of loss. And certainly, money doesn't solve the challenges that might arise with losing someone important.

It has been said that when you have money, you have options. When you don't have money, your options are severely limited. You might imagine a life insurance policy can give your family and loved ones options that would otherwise be impossible.

> » *Ben spent the last 20 years building a small business. In so many ways, it is a family business. Each of his three children, Maddie, Ruby and Edward, worked in the shop part-time during high school. But after all three attended college, only Maddie returned to join her father, and eventually will run the business full-time when Ben retires.*
>
> *Ben is able to retire comfortably on Social Security and on-going income from the shop, but the business is nearly his entire financial legacy. It is his wish that Maddie own the business outright, but he also wants to leave an equal legacy to each of his three children.*
>
> *There is no simple way to divide the business into thirds and still leave the business intact for Maddie.*
>
> *Ben ends up buying a life insurance policy to make up the difference. Ruby and Edward will receive their share of an inheritance in cash from the life insurance policy and Maddie will be able to inherit the business intact.*
>
> *Ben is able to accomplish his goals, treat all three children equitably and leave Maddie the business she helped to build.*

If you have a life insurance policy but you haven't looked at it in a while, you may not know how it operates, how much it is worth and how it will be distributed to your beneficiaries. You may also need to update your beneficiaries on your policy. In short, without a comprehensive review of your policy, you don't really know where the money will go or to whom it will go.

If you don't have a life insurance policy but are looking for options to maintain and grow your legacy, speaking with a professional can show you the benefits of life insurance. Many people don't consider buying a life insurance policy until some event in their life triggers it, like the loss of a loved one, an accident or a health condition.

BENEFITS OF LIFE INSURANCE

Life insurance is a useful and secure tool for contingency planning, ensuring that your dependents receive the assets that you want them to have, and for meeting the financial goals you have set for the future. While it bears the name "Life Insurance," it is, in reality, a diverse financial tool that can meet many needs. Today's life insurance policies offer what are known as Living Benefits. These benefits provide the insuree additional income while they are still alive should the need arise due to chronic illness or the cost of long term care. Traditionally, the main function of a life insurance policy is to provide financial assets for your survivors. Life insurance is particularly efficient at achieving this goal because it provides a tax-advantaged lump sum of money in the form of a death benefit to your beneficiary or beneficiaries. That financial asset can be used in a number of ways. It can be structured as an investment to provide income for your spouse or children, it can pay down debts, and it can be used to cover estate taxes and other costs associated with death.

Tax liabilities on the estate you leave behind are inevitable. Capital property, for instance, is taxed at its fair market value at the time of your death, unless that property is transferred to your spouse. If the property has appreciated during the time you owned it, taxation on capital gains will occur. Registered Retirement Savings Plans (RRSPs) and other similarly structured assets are also included as taxable income unless transferred to a beneficiary as well. Those are just a few examples of how an estate can become subject to a heavy tax burden. The unique benefits of a life insurance policy provide ways to handle this tax burden, solving any liquidity problems that may arise if your family members want to hold onto an illiquid asset, such as a piece of property or an investment. Life insurance can provide a significant amount of money to a family member or other beneficiary, and that money is likely to remain exempt from taxation or seizure.

One of life insurance's most important benefits is that it is not considered part of the estate of the policy holder. The death benefit that is paid by the insurance company goes exclusively to the beneficiaries listed on the policy. This shields the proceeds of the policy from fees and costs that can reduce an estate, including probate proceedings, attorneys' fees and claims made by creditors. The distribution of your life insurance policy is also unaffected by delays of the estate's distribution, like probate. Your beneficiaries will get the proceeds of the policy in a timely fashion, regardless of how long it takes for the rest of your estate to be settled.

Investing a portion of your assets in a life insurance policy can also protect that portion of your estate from creditors. If you owe money to someone or some entity at the time of your death, a creditor is not able to claim any money from a life insurance policy or an annuity, for that matter (unless you have already used the life insurance policy as collateral against a loan). If a large portion of the money you want to dedicate to your legacy is sitting in a savings account, investment or other liquid form, creditors may be able to receive their claim on it before your beneficiaries get anything, that is if there's anything left. A life insurance policy protects your assets from creditors and ensures that your beneficiaries get the money that you intend them to have.

HOW MUCH LIFE INSURANCE DO YOU NEED?

Determining the type of policy and the amount right for you depends on an analysis of your needs. A financial professional can help you complete a needs analysis that will highlight the amount of insurance that you require to meet your goals. This type of personalized review will allow you to determine ways to continue providing income for your spouse or any dependents you may have. A financial professional can also help you calculate the amount of income that your policy should replace to meet the needs of your beneficiaries and the duration of the distribution of that income.

You may also want to use your life insurance policy to meet any expenses associated with your death. These can include funeral costs, fees from probate and legal proceedings, and taxes. You may also want to dedicate a portion of your policy proceeds to help fund tuition or other expenses for your children or grandchildren. You can buy a policy and hope it covers all of those costs, or you can work with a professional who can calculate exactly how much insurance you need and how to structure it to meet your goals. Which would you rather do?

AVOIDING POTENTIAL SNAGS

There are benefits to having life insurance that supersede the direction given in a will or other estate plan, but there are also some potential snags that you should address to meet your wishes. For example, if your will instructs that your assets be divided equally between your two children but your life insurance beneficiary is listed as just one of the children, the assets in the life insurance policy will only be distributed to the child listed as the beneficiary. The beneficiary designation of your life insurance supersedes your will's instruction. This is important to understand when designating beneficiaries on a policy you purchase. Work with a professional to make sure that your beneficiaries are accurately listed on your assets, especially your life insurance policies.

USING LIFE INSURANCE TO BUILD YOUR LEGACY

Depending on your goals, there are strategies you can use that could multiply how much you leave behind. Life insurance is one of the most surefire and efficient investment tools for building a substantial legacy that will meet your financial goals.

Here is a brief overview of how life insurance can boost your legacy:

- Life insurance provides an immediate increase in your legacy.
- It provides an income tax-advantaged death benefit for your beneficiaries.
- A good life insurance policy has the opportunity to accumulate value over time.
- Some life insurance policies have an option to include long-term care (LTC) or chronic illness benefits should you require them.

If your income needs for retirement are met and you have Orange Money assets that will provide for your future expenses, you may have extra assets that you want to earmark as legacy funds. By electing to invest those assets into a life insurance policy, you can immediately increase the amount of your legacy. Remember, **life insurance allows you to transfer a tax-advantaged lump sum of money to your beneficiaries. It remains in your control during your lifetime, can provide for your long-term care needs and bypasses probate costs.** And make no mistake, taxes can have a huge impact on your legacy. Not only that, income and assets from your legacy can have tax implications for your beneficiaries, as well.

Here's a brief overview of how taxes could affect your legacy and your beneficiaries:

- The higher your income, the higher the rate at which it is taxed.
- Withdrawals from qualified plans are taxed as income.
- What's more, when you leave a large qualified plan, it ends up being taxed at a high rate.
- If you left a $500,000 IRA to your child, they could end up owing as much as $140,000 in income taxes.
- However, if you could just withdraw $50,000 a year, the tax bill might only be $10,000 per year.

How could you use that annual amount to leave a larger legacy? Luckily, you can leverage a life insurance policy to avoid those tax penalties, preserving a larger amount of your legacy and freeing your beneficiaries from an added tax burden.

> » *When Lettie turned 70 years old, she decided it was time to look into life insurance policy options. She still feels young, but she remembers that her mother died in her early 70s, and she wants to plan ahead so she can pass on some of her legacy to her grandchildren just like her grandmother did for her.*
>
> *Lettie doesn't really want to think about life insurance, but she does want the security, reliability and tax-advantaged distribution that it offers. She lives modestly, and her Social Security benefit meets most of her income needs. As the beneficiary of her late husband's Certificate of Deposit (CD), she has $100,000 in an account that she has never used and doesn't anticipate ever needing since her income needs were already met.*
>
> *After looking at several different investment options with a professional, Lettie decides that a Single Premium life insurance policy fits her needs best. She can buy the policy*

with a $100,000 one-time payment and she is guaranteed that it would provide more than the value of the contract to her beneficiaries. If she left the money in the CD, it would be subject to taxes, but for every dollar that she puts into the life insurance policy, her beneficiaries are guaranteed at least that dollar plus a death benefit, and all of it will be **tax-free!**

For $100,000, Lettie's particular policy offers a $170,000 death benefit distribution to her beneficiaries. By moving the $100,000 from a CD to a life insurance policy, Lettie increases her legacy by 70 percent. Not only that, she has also sheltered it from taxes, so her beneficiaries will be able to receive $1.70 for every $1.00 that she entered into the policy! While buying the policy doesn't allow her to use the money for herself, it does allow her family to benefit from her well-planned legacy.

MAKE YOUR WISHES KNOWN

Estate taxes used to be a much hotter topic in the mid-2000s when the estate tax limits and exclusions were much smaller and taxed at a higher rate than today. In 2008, estates valued at $2 million or more were taxed at 45 percent. Just two years later, the limit was raised to $5 million dollars taxed at 35 percent. The limit has continued to rise ever since. The limit applies to fewer people than before. Estate organization, however, is just as important as ever, and it affects everyone.

Ask yourself:

- Are your assets actually titled and held the way you think they are?
- Are your beneficiaries set up the way you think they should be?
- Have there been changes to your family or those you desire as beneficiaries?

There is more to your legacy beyond your property, money, investments and other assets that you leave to family members, loved ones and charities. Everyone has a legacy beyond money. You also leave behind personal items of importance, your values and beliefs, your personal and family history, and your wishes. Beyond a will and a plan for your assets, it is important that you make your wishes known to someone for the rest of your personal legacy. When it comes time for your family and loved ones to make decisions after you are gone, knowing your wishes can help them make decisions that honor you and your legacy, and give meaning to what you leave behind. Your professional can help you organize.

Think about your:

- Personal stories / recollections
- Values
- Personal items of emotional significance
- Financial assets

Do you want to make a plan to pass these things on to your family?

Venturing into the jungle of policies, brokers and salespeople can be overwhelming, and can leave you wondering if you've made the best decision. Working with a trusted financial professional can help you cut through the red tape, the "sales-speak" and confusion to find a policy that meets your goals and best serves your desires for your money. If you already have a policy, a financial professional can help you review it and become familiar with the policy's premium, the guarantees the policy affords, its performance, and its features and benefits. A financial professional can also help you make any necessary changes.

HOW DO YOU FIND A TRUE ESTATE PLANNING ATTORNEY?

When searching for an estate planning attorney, look for financial professionals who recommend the services of a trusted colleague or who employ an estate planning attorney as part of their firm. Professionals who have your best interests at heart will have an estate planning attorney available who can make sure your intentions are honored. George and Dee Booth in our opening story did find a professional, but their intentions were not honored. When hiring an estate attorney, make sure the attorney does the following three things:

- They understand the power of using a Living Trust.
- They understand the power and importance of avoiding probate.
- They ask to see all of your deeds, accounts and beneficiary designations.

Things change, relationships evolve and the way you would like your legacy organized needs to adapt to the changes that happen throughout your life. There may be a new child or grandchild in your family or you may have been divorced or remarried. A professional will regularly review your legacy assets and ask you questions to make sure that everything is up to date and that the current organization reflects your current wishes.

CHAPTER 11 RECAP //

- You can structure your assets in ways that maximize distributions and decrease taxes to your beneficiaries. Working with a financial professional can help you design a plan that best meets your retirement goals and helps you avoid the ponderous and expensive probate process.

- A financial professional can help review the details of the assets you have designated to be a part of your legacy and make sure that you aren't unintentionally disinheriting your heirs.

- Life insurance provides for the distribution of tax-free, liquid assets to your beneficiaries and can significantly build your legacy. They can also provide Living Benefits to help you pay for the high costs of medical care while you are still living.

- You can take advantage of a "Stretch IRA" to provide income for you, your spouse and your beneficiaries throughout their lifetimes.

- To avoid unintentional disinheritance, understand the difference between the designations *per stirpes* and *per capita* and make sure that all your paperwork is coordinated to reflect your intentions.

12

How Do I Find the Right Financial Professional?

Who do you trust with your money?

Marlin found out that his wife, Gloria, had an aggressive form of stomach cancer. Gloria had a very good doctor whom she had been seeing since she was a child, but Marlin wanted his wife to have the best treatment possible in order to improve her chances for recovery. Instead of taking her to their local clinic, Marlin asked around. He talked to friends, family and colleagues. He cross-referenced those recommendations with information he found online. He made phone calls, read books and did all the research he could to make sure that his wife got the very best professional for the job. Marlin brought his wife to a professional who specialized in the exact type of cancer that Gloria had, and that professional started her on a customized course of treatment.

167

While seeking the help of a financial professional to coordinate your retirement income is rarely a life-or-death decision, it does represent a specialized field. Just as the doctor who does family check-ups down the street is not qualified to operate on your spinal cord, so, too, the broker who sold you your mutual funds may not be qualified to guide you through the retirement income planning process. There are many people that would love to handle your money, but not everyone is qualified to handle it in a way that leads to a holistic approach to creating a solid retirement plan.

The distinction being made here is that you should look for someone that puts your interests first and actively wants to help you meet your goals and objectives. Oftentimes, the products someone sells you matter less than their dedication to making sure that you have a plan that meets your needs.

Professionals take your whole financial position into consideration. They make plans that adjust your risk exposure, invest in tools that secure your desired income during retirement and create investment strategies that allow you to continue accumulating wealth during your retirement for you to use later or to contribute to your legacy. If you buy stocks with a broker, use a different agent for a life insurance policy and have an unmanaged 401(k) through your employer, working with a financial professional will consolidate the management of your assets so you have one trustworthy person quarterbacking all of the team elements of your portfolio. Financial products and investment tools change, but the concepts that lie behind wise retirement planning are lasting. In the end, a financial professional's approach is designed for those serious about planning for retirement. *Can you say the same thing about the person that advises you about your financial life?*

It's easy to see how choosing a financial professional can be one of the most important decisions you can make in your life. Not only do they provide you with advice, they also manage the personal assets that supply your retirement income and contribute to your legacy. So, how do you find a good one?

HOW TO FIND A FINANCIAL PROFESSIONAL YOU CAN TRUST

Taking care to select a financial professional is one of the best things you can do for yourself and for your future. Your professional has influence and control of your investment decisions, making their role in your life more than just important. Your financial security and the quality of your retirement depend on the decisions, investment strategies and asset structuring that you and your professional create.

Working with a professional is different than calling up a broker when you want to buy or trade some stock. This isn't a decision that you can hand off to anyone else. You need to bring your time and attention to the table when it comes to finding someone with whom you can entrust your financial life. Separating the wheat from the chaff will take some work, but you'll be happy you did it.

While no one can tell you exactly who to choose or how to choose them, the following information can help you narrow the field:

- You can start by asking your friends, family and colleagues for referrals. You will want to pay particular attention to the recommendations that you get from others who are in your similar financial situation and who have similar lifestyle choices. The financial professional for the CEO of your company may have a different skill-set than the skill-set of the professional helping your cousin who has three kids and a Subaru like you. Do follow-up research on the Internet as well. Look up the people who have been recommended to you on websites like LinkedIn that show the work history, referrals and experience of the candidates that you find most attractive. You will also learn about the firms with or for whom they work. The investment philosophies and reputations of the companies they work for will tell you a lot about how they will handle your money.

- The other side of the coin, however, is that everyone and their brother has a recommendation about how you should manage your money and who should manage it for you. From hot stock tips to "the best money manager in the state," people love to share information that makes them look like they are in-the-know. Nobody wants to talk about the bad stock purchases they made, the times they lost money and the poor selections they made regarding financial professionals or stock brokers. If you decide to take a friend or family member's recommendation, make sure they have a substantial, long-term experience with the financial professional and that their glowing review isn't just based on a one-time "win."

- Many professionals may also be brokers or dealers that can earn commissions on things like life insurance, certain types of annuities and disability insurance. These professionals have most likely intentionally overlapped their roles so that if their clients choose to purchase insurance or investment products that require a broker or dealer, those clients won't have to find an additional person to work with. Again, understanding the role of your professional will help you make your determination.

NARROWING THE FIELD

1. Decide on the Type of Professional with Whom You Want to Work. There are four basic kinds of financial professionals. Many professionals may play overlapping roles. It is important to know a professional's primary function, how they charge for their services and whether they are obligated to act in your best interest.

Registered representatives, better known as stockbrokers or bank/ investment representatives, make their living by earning commissions on insurance products and investment services. Stockbrokers basically sell you things. The products from which they make the highest commission are sometimes the products that they recommend to their clients. If you want to make a simple transaction, such as buying or selling a particular stock, a registered representative can help you. Although registered representatives are licensed professionals, if you want to create a structured and planful approach to positioning your assets for retirement, you might want to consider continuing your search. In addition, their license only requires them to "do no harm" for their clients, as opposed to having any type of fiduciary responsibility to do what is best.

The term "planner" is often misused. It can refer to credible professionals that are CPAs, CFPs and ChFCs to your uncle's next door neighbor who claims to have a lead on some undervalued stock about to be "discovered." A wide array of people may claim to be planners because there are no requirements to be a planner. The term financial planner, however, refers to someone who is properly registered as an investment advisor and serves as a fiduciary as described below.

Financial professionals are the diamonds in the rough. These *Registered Investment Advisors* are compensated on a fee basis. They do, however, often have licensure as stockbrokers or insurance agents, allowing them to earn commissions on certain transactions. More importantly, **financial professionals are financial fiduciaries, meaning they are required to make financial decisions in your best interest and reflecting your risk tolerance.** Investment Advisors are held to higher ethical standards and are highly regarded in the financial industry. Financial professionals also often take a more comprehensive approach to asset management. These professionals are trained and credentialed to plan and coordinate their clients' assets in order to meet their goals or retirement and legacy planning. They are not focused on individual stocks, investments or markets. They look at the big picture, the whole enchilada.

Money managers are on par with financial professionals. However, they are often given explicit permission to make investment decisions without advanced approval by their clients.

Understanding who you are working with and what their title is the first step to planning your retirement. While each of the above-mentioned types of financial professionals can help you with aspects of your finances, it is holistic **financial professionals** who have the most intimate role, the most objective investment strategies and the most unbiased mode of compensation for their services. A financial professional can also help you with the non-financial aspects of your legacy and can help you find ways to create a tax planning strategy to help you save money.

2. Be Objective. At the end of the day, you need to separate the weak from the strong. While you might want a strong personal rapport with your professional, or you may want to choose your professional for their personality and positive attitude, it is more important that you find someone who will give sage advice regarding achieving your retirement goals.

It can be helpful to use a process of elimination to narrow the field of potential professionals. Look into five or six potential leads and cross off your list the ones that don't meet your requirements until only one or two remain. Cross-check your remaining choices against the list of things you need from a professional. Make sure they represent a firm that has the investment tools and products that you desire, and make sure they have experience in retirement planning. That is, after all, the main goal.

Don't be afraid to investigate each of your candidates. You'll want to ask the same questions and look for the same information from everyone you consider so you can then compare them and discern which is best for you. You'll want to take a look at the specific credentials of each professional, their experience and competence, their ethics and fiduciary status, their history and track record, and a list of the services that they offer. The professionals who meet all or most of your qualifications are the ones you will contact for an interview.

Potential professionals should meet your qualifications in the following categories:

- *Credentials:* Look at their experience, the quality of their education, any associations to which they belong and certifications they have earned. Someone who has continued their professional education through ongoing certifications will be more up-to-date on current financial practices compared to someone who got their degree 25 years ago and hasn't done a thing since.
- *Practices:* Look at the track record of your candidates, how they are compensated for their services, the reports and analysis they offer, and their value added services.
- *Services:* Your professional must meet your needs. If you are planning your retirement, you should work with someone who offers services that help you to that end. You want someone who can offer planning, advice on investment strategies, ways to calculate risk, advice on insurance and annuities products, and ways to manage your tax strategy.
- *Ethics:* You want to work with someone who is above board and does things the right way. Vet them by checking their compliance record, current licensing, fiduciary status and, yes, even their criminal record. You never know!

3. Ask for and Check References. Once you have selected two or three professionals that you want to meet, call or email them and ask for references. Every professional should be able to provide you with at least two or three names. In fact, they will probably be eager to share them with you. Most professionals rely on references for validation of their success, quality of services and likability.

Ask each reference the same set of questions to get the same basic information. How long have they been working with the professional? What kind of services have they used and were they happy with them? What type of financial planning did they use the professional for? Were they versed in the type of financial planning that you needed? You can also ask them direct questions to elicit candid responses. What was the full cost of the expenses that your professional charged you? Do the reports and statements you receive come from the same firm? Questions like these can help you get a sense of how well the reference knows their professional and whether or not they are a quality reference.

A good reference is a bit like icing on the cake. It's nice to have them, but nothing speaks louder than a good track record and quality experience. And remember that a good reference, while nice to hear, is relatively cheap. How many times have you heard someone on the golf course or at work telling you how great their stockbroker is? But how many times have you heard about the bad investments or losses they have experienced?

HOW TO INTERVIEW CANDIDATES

After vetting your candidates and narrowing down a list of professionals that you think might be a good fit for you, it's time to start interviewing.

When you meet in person with a professional, you want to take advantage of your time with them. The presentations and information that they share with you will be important to pay attention to, but you will also want to control some aspects of the interview. After a professional has told you what they want you to hear, it's time to ask your own questions to get the specific information you need to make your decision.

Make sure to prepare a list of questions and an informal agenda so that you can keep track of what you want to ask and what points you want the professional to touch on during the interview. Using the same questions and agenda will also allow you to more easily compare the professionals after you have interviewed them all. Remember that these interviews are just that, *interviews*. You are meeting with several professionals to determine with whom you want to work. Don't agree to anything or sign anything during an interview until after you have made your final decision.

It can also be helpful to put a time limit on your interviews and to meet the professionals at their offices. The time limit will keep things on track and will allow structured time for presentations and questions/discussion. By meeting them at their office, you can get a sense of the work environment, the staff culture and attitude, and how the firm does business. If you are unable to travel to a professional's office and must meet them at your home or office, make sure that your interviews are scheduled with plenty of time between so the professionals don't cross each other's paths.

You can use the following questions during an initial interview to get an understanding of how each professional does business and whether they are a good fit for you.

1. How do you charge for your services? How much do you charge? This information should be easy to find on their website, but if you don't see it, ask. Find out if they charge an initial planning fee, if they charge a percentage for assets under their management and if they make money by selling specific financial products or services. If so, you should follow up by asking how much the service costs. This will give you an idea of how they really make their money and if they have incentive to sell certain products over others. Make sure you understand exactly how you will be charged so there are no surprises down the road if you decide to work with this person.

2. What are your credentials, licenses, and certifications? There are Chartered Financial Consultants (ChFCs), Investment Advisor Representatives, Certified Public Accountants (CPAs) and Personal Financial Specialists (PFSs). Whatever their credentials or titles, you want to be sure that the professional you work with is an expert in the field relevant to your circumstances. If you want someone to manage your money, you will most likely look for a Registered Investment Advisor. Someone that works with an independent firm will likely have a team of CPAs, CFPs and other financial experts upon whom they can draw. If you like the professional you are meeting with and you think they might be a good fit, but they don't have the accounting experience you want them to have, ask about their firm and the resources available to them. If they work closely with CPAs that are experienced in your needs, it could be a good match.

3. What are the financial services that you and your firm provide? The question within the question here is, "Can you help me achieve my goals?" Some people can only provide you with investment advice, and others are tax consultants. You will likely want to work with someone that provides a complete suite of financial planning services and products that touch on retirement planning, Social Security maximization, insurance options, legacy and estate structuring, and tax planning. There are also non-financial issues such as longevity, Medicare and long term care insurance. A good plan will take into account life situations and the big picture, and will factor those in right along with the numbers.

Whatever services they provide, make sure they meet both your needs and your anticipated needs.

4. What kinds of clients do you work with the most? A lot of financial professionals work within a niche: retirement planning, risk assessment, life insurance, etc. Finding someone who works with other people that are in the same financial boat as you and who have similar goals can be an important way to make sure they understand your needs. While someone might be a crackerjack annuities cowboy, you might not be interested in that option. Ask follow-up questions that will really help you understand where their expertise lies and whether or not their experience lines up with your needs.

5. May I see a sample of one of your financial plans? You wouldn't buy a car without test driving it, and you should not work with a professional without seeing a sample of how they do business. While there is no formal structure that a financial plan has to follow, the variation between professionals can help you find someone who "speaks your language." One professional may provide you with an in-depth analysis that relies heavily on info graphics and diagrams. Someone else may give you a seven page review of your assets and general recommendations. By seeing a sample plan, you can narrow down who presents information in the way that you desire and in ways that you understand.

6. How do you approach investing? You may be entirely in the dark about how to approach your investments, or you might have some guiding principles. Either way, ask each candidate what their philosophy is. Some will resonate with you and some won't. A good professional who has a realistic approach to investing won't promise you the moon or tell you that they can make you a lot of money. Professionals who are successful at retirement planning and full service financial management will tell you that they will listen to your goals, risk tolerance and comfort level with different types of investment strategies. Working with someone that you trust is critical, and this question in particular can help you find out who you can and who you can't.

7. How do you remain in contact with your clients? Does your prospective professional hold annual, quarterly or monthly meetings? How often do *you* want to meet with your professional? Some people want to check in once a year, go over everything and make sure their ducks are all in a row. If any changes over the previous year or additions to their legacy planning strategy came up, they'll do it on that date. Other people want a monthly update to be more involved in the decision making process and to understand what's happening with their portfolio. You basically need to determine the right degree of involvement for both you and your financial professional. You'll also want to feel out how your professional communicates. Do you prefer phone calls or face-to-face meetings? Do you want your professional to explain things to you in detail or to summarize for you what decisions they've made? Is the professional willing to give you their direct phone number or their email address? More importantly, do you want that information and do you want to be able to contact them in those ways?

8. Are you my main contact, or do you work with a team? This is another way of finding out how involved with you your professional will be, and how often they will meet with you. It is also a way to discover how the firm they represent operates and manages their clients. Some professionals will answer their own phone, meet with you regularly and have your home phone number on speed dial. Others will meet with you once a year and have a partner or assistant check in with you every quarter to give you an update. Other companies take an entirely team-based approach whereby clients have a main contact but their portfolio is handled by a team of professionals that represent the firm. One way isn't better than another, but one way will be best for you. Find out how the professional you are interviewing operates before entering into an agreement.

9. How do you provide a unique experience for your clients?
This is a polite way of asking, "Why should I work with you?"
A professional should have a compelling answer to this question
that connects with you. Their answer will likely touch on their
investment philosophy, their communication style and their
expertise. If you hear them describing strengths and philosophies
that resonate with you, keep them on your list. Some professionals will tell you that they will make investments with your money
that match your values, others will say they will maximize your
returns and others will say they will protect your capital while
structuring your assets for income. Whatever you're looking for
in a professional, you will most likely find it in the answer to this
question.

This last question you will want to ask *yourself* after you've met
with someone who you are considering hiring:

**10. Did they ask questions and show signs that they were in-
terested in working with me?** A professional who will structure
your assets to reflect your risk tolerance and to position you for a
comfortable retirement must be a good listener. You will want to
pass by a professional who talks non-stop and tells you what to do
without listening to what you want them to do. If you felt they
listened well and understood your needs, and seemed interested
and experienced in your situation, then they might be right for
you.

THE IMPORTANCE OF INDEPENDENCE
Not all investment firms and financial professionals are created
equal. The information in this book has systematically shown that
leveraging investments for income and accumulation in today's
market requires new ideas and modern planning. In short, you
need innovative ideas to come up with the creative solutions

that will provide you with the retirement that you want. Innovation thrives on independence. No matter how good a financial professional is, the firm that they represent needs to operate on principles that make sense in today's economy. Remember, advice about money has been around forever. Good advice, however, changes with the times.

Timing the market, relying on the sale of stocks for income and banking on high treasury and bond returns are not strategies. They aren't even realistic ways to make money or to generate income. Working with an independent planner can help you break free from the old ways of thinking and position you to create a realistic retirement plan.

Working with an independent professional who relies on fee-based income tied to the success of their performance will also give you greater peace of mind. When you do well, they do well, and that's the way it should be. Your independent financial professional will make sure that:

- Your assets are organized and structured to reflect your risk tolerance.
- Your assets will be available to you when you need them and in the way that you need them.
- You will have a lifetime income that will support your lifestyle through your retirement.
- You are handling your taxes as efficiently as possible.
- Your legacy is in order.
- Your Red Money is turned into Orange Money, and is managed in your best interest.

IT'S WORTH IT!

Finding, interviewing and selecting a financial professional can seem like a daunting task. And honestly, it will take a good amount of work to narrow the field and find the one you want. In the end, it is worth the blood, sweat and tears. Your retirement, lifestyle, assets and legacy is on the line. The choices you make today will have lasting impacts on your life and the life of your loved ones. Working with someone you trust and know you can rely on to make decisions that will benefit you is invaluable. The work it takes to find them is something you will never regret.

Here is a recap of why working with a financial professional is the best retirement decision you can make:

CHAPTER 12 RECAP //

- A good financial professional puts your needs and happiness first. Your risk tolerance, goals, objectives, needs, wants, liquidity concerns and timeline worries should be the focus of the meeting before they try to sell you any products. A good plan must also be revisited to make sure it is still a good fit for your current life situation.
- Finding a financial professional you can trust is imperative, because money isn't just about numbers; it's about the life events and the people that come attached to those numbers.
- To find a professional you can trust, start by asking family and friends for referrals. Make sure to do your due diligence and check out the references of anyone who is recommended to you.
- When interviewing candidates, make sure you understand how they charge for their services. Also look for credentials, licenses and certifications. Ask questions such as: How often do you check in with your clients? Do you offer a Social Security Optimization report? May I see a sample of one of your financial plans? And How do you approach investing? These questions will help ensure that you and your professional are a good fit for each other.

Glossary

ANNUAL RESET *(ANNUAL RATCHET, CLIQUET)* – Crediting methods measuring index movement over a one year period. Positive interest is calculated and credited at the end of each contract year and cannot be lost if the index subsequently declines. Say that the index increased from 100 to 110 in one year and the indexed annuity had an 80 percent participation rate. The insurance company would take the 10 percent gross index gain for the year (110-100/100), apply the participation rate (10 percent index gain x 80 percent rate) and credit 8 percent interest to the annuity. But, what if in the following year the index declined back to 100? The individual would keep the 8 percent interest earned and simply receive zero interest for the down year. An annual reset structure preserves credited gains and treats negative index periods as years with zero growth.

ANNUITANT – The person, usually the annuity owner, whose life expectancy is used to calculate the income payment amount on the annuity.

ANNUITY – An annuity is a contract issued by an insurance company that often serves as a type of savings plan used by individuals looking for long term growth and protection of assets that will likely be needed within retirement.

AVERAGING – Index values may either be measured from a start point to an end point (point-to-point) or values between the start point and end point may be averaged to determine an ending value. Index values may be averaged over the days, weeks, months or quarters of the period.

BENEFICIARY – A beneficiary is the person designated to receive payments due upon the death of the annuity owner or the annuitant themselves.

BONUS RATE – A bonus rate is the "extra" or "additional" interest paid during the first year (the initial guarantee period), typically used as an added incentive to get consumers to select their annuity policy over another.

CALL OPTION *(ALSO SEE PUT OPTION)* – Gives the holder the right to buy an underlying security or index at a specified price on or before a given date.

CAP – The maximum interest rate that will be credited to the annuity for the year or period. The cap usually refers to the maximum interest credited after applying the participation rate or yield spread. If the index methodology showed a 20 percent increase, the participation rate was 60 percent and the maximum interest cap was 10 percent, the contract would credit 10 percent interest. A few annuities use a maximum gain cap instead of a maximum interest cap with the participation rate or yield spread applied to the lesser of the gain or the cap. If the index methodology showed a 20 percent increase, the participation rate was 60 percent and the maximum gain cap was 10 percent, the contract would credit 6 percent interest.

COMPOUND INTEREST – Interest is earned on both the original principal and on previously earned interest. It is more favorable than simple interest. Suppose that your original principal was $1 and your interest rate was 10 percent for five years. With simple interest, your value is ($1 + $0.10 interest each year) = $1.50. With compound interest, your value is ($1 x 1.10 x 1.10 x 1.10 x 1.10 x 1.10) = $1.61. The advantage of compound interest over simple interest becomes greater as each subsequent period passes.

CREDITING METHOD *(ALSO SEE METHODOLOGY)* – The formula(s) used to determine the excess interest that is credited above the minimum interest guarantee.

DEATH BENEFITS – The payment the annuity owner's estate or beneficiaries will receive if he or she dies before the annuity matures. On most annuities, this is equal to the current account value. Some annuities offer an enhanced value at death via an optional rider that has a monthly or annual fee associated with it.

EXCESS INTEREST – Interest credited to the annuity contract above the minimum guaranteed interest rate. In an indexed annuity the excess interest is determined by applying a stated crediting method to a specific index or indices.

FIXED ANNUITY – A contract issued by an insurance company guaranteeing a minimum interest rate with the crediting of excess interest determined by the performance of the insurer's general account. Index annuities are fixed annuities.

FIXED DEFERRED ANNUITY – With fixed annuities, an insurance company offers a guaranteed interest rate plus safety of your principal and earnings ((subject to the claims-paying ability of the insurance company). Your interest rate will be reset periodically, based on economic and other factors, but is guaranteed to never fall below a certain rate.

FREE WITHDRAWALS – Withdrawals that are free of surrender charges.

INDEX – The underlying external benchmark upon which the crediting of excess interest is based, also a measure of the prices of a group of securities.

IRA *(INDIVIDUAL RETIREMENT ACCOUNT)* – An IRA is a tax-advantaged personal savings plan that lets an individual set aside money for retirement. All or part of the participant's contributions may be tax deductible, depending on the type of IRA chosen and the participant's personal financial circumstances. Distributions from many employer-sponsored retirement plans may be eligible to be rolled into an IRA to continue tax-deferred growth until the funds are needed. An annuity can be used as an IRA; that is, IRA funds can be used to purchase an annuity.

IRA ROLLOVER – IRA rollover is the phrase used when an individual who has a balance in an employer-sponsored retirement plan transfers that balance into an IRA. Such an exchange, when properly handled, is a tax-advantaged transaction.

LIQUIDITY – The ease with which an asset is convertible to cash. An asset with high liquidity provides flexibility, in that the owner can easily convert it to cash at any time, but it also tends to decrease profitability.

MARKET RISK – The risk of the market value of an asset fluctuating up or down over time. In a fixed or fixed indexed annuity, the original principal and credited interest are not subject to market risk. Even if the index declines, the annuity owner would receive no less than their original principal back if they decided to cash in the policy at the end of the surrender period. Unlike a security, indexed annuities guarantee the original premium and the premium is backed by, and is as safe as, the insurance company that issued it (subject to the claims-paying ability of the insurance company).

METHODOLOGY *(ALSO SEE CREDITING METHOD)* – The way that interest crediting is calculated. On fixed indexed annuities, there are a variety of different methods used to determine how index movement becomes interest credited.

MINIMUM GUARANTEED RETURN *(MINIMUM INTEREST RATE)* – Fixed indexed annuities typically provide a minimum guaranteed return over the life of the contract. At the time that the owner chooses to terminate the contract, the cash surrender value is compared to a second value calculated using the minimum guaranteed return and the higher of the two values is paid to the annuity owner.

OPTION – A contract which conveys to its holder the right, but not the obligation, to buy or sell something at a specified price on or before a given date. After this given date the option ceases to exist. Insurers typically buy options to provide for the excess interest potential. Options may be American style whereby they

may be exercised at any time prior to the given date, or they may
have to be exercised only during a specified window. Options that
may only be exercised during a specified period are European-
style options.

OPTION RISK – Most insurers create the potential for excess
interest in an indexed annuity by buying options. Say that you
could buy a share of stock for $50. If you bought the stock and
it rose to $60 you could sell it and net a $10 profit. But, if the
stock price fell to $40 you'd have a $10 loss. Instead of buying the
actual stock, we could buy an option that gave us the right to buy
the stock for $50 at any time over the next year. The cost of the
option is $2. If the stock price rose to $60 we would exercise our
option, buy the stock at $50 and make $10 (less the $2 cost of
the option). If the price of the stock fell to $40, $30 or $10, we
wouldn't use the option and it would expire. The loss is limited to
$2 – the cost of the option.

PARTICIPATION RATE – The percentage of positive index
movement credited to the annuity. If the index methodology
determined that the index increased 10 percent and the indexed
annuity participated in 60 percent of the increase, it would be said
that the contract has a 60 percent participation rate. Participation
rates may also be expressed as asset fees or yield spreads.

POINT-TO-POINT – A crediting method measuring index movement from an absolute initial point to the absolute end point for a
period. An index had a period starting value of 100 and a period
ending value of 120. A point-to-point method would record a
positive index movement of 20 [120-100] or a 20 percent positive
movement [(120-100)/100]. Point-to-point usually refers to annual periods; however the phrase is also used instead of term end
point to refer to multiple year periods.

PREMIUM BONUS – A premium bonus is additional money that is credited to the accumulation account of an annuity policy under certain conditions.

PUT OPTION *(ALSO SEE CALL OPTION)* – Gives the holder the right to sell an underlying security or index at a specified price on or before a given date.

QUALIFIED ANNUITIES *(QUALIFIED MONEY)* – Qualified annuities are annuities purchased for funding an IRA, 403(b) tax-deferred annuity or other type of retirement arrangements. An IRA or qualified retirement plan provides the tax deferral. An annuity contract should be used to fund an IRA or qualified retirement plan to benefit from an annuity's features other than tax deferral, including the safety features, lifetime income payout option and death benefit protection.

REQUIRED MINIMUM DISTRIBUTION *(RMD)* – The amount of money that Traditional, SEP and SIMPLE IRA owners and qualified plan participants must begin distributing from their retirement accounts by April 1 following the year they reach age 70.5. RMD amounts must then be distributed each subsequent year.

RETURN FLOOR – Another way of saying minimum guaranteed return.

ROTH IRA – Like other IRA accounts, the Roth IRA is simply a holding account that manages your stocks, bonds, annuities, mutual funds and CD's. However, future withdrawals (including earnings and interest) are typically tax-advantaged once the account has been open for five years and the account holder is age 59.5.

RULE OF 72 – Tells you approximately how many years it takes a sum to double at a given rate. It's handy to be able to figure out, without using a calculator, that when you're earning a 6 percent return, for example, by dividing 6 percent into 72, you'll find that it takes 12 years for money to double. Conversely, if you know it took a sum twelve years to double you could divide 12 into 72 to determine the annual return (6 percent).

SIMPLE INTEREST *(ALSO SEE COMPOUND INTEREST)* – Interest is only earned on the principal balance.

SPLIT ANNUITY – A split annuity is the term given to an effective strategy that utilizes two or more different annuity products – one designed to generate monthly income and the other to restore the original starting principal over a set period of time.

STANDARD & POOR'S 500 *(S&P 500)* – The most widely used external index by fixed indexed annuities. Its objective is to be a benchmark to measure and report overall U.S. stock market performance. It includes a representative sample of 500 common stocks from companies trading on the New York Stock Exchange, American Stock Exchange, and NASDAQ National Market System. The index represents the price or market value of the underlying stocks and does not include the value of reinvested dividends of the underlying stocks.

STOCK MARKET INDEX – A report created from a type of statistical measurement that shows up or down changes in a specific financial market, usually expressed as points and as a percentage, in a number of related markets, or in an economy as a whole (i.e. S&P 500 or New York Stock Exchange).

SURRENDER CHARGE – A charge imposed for withdrawing funds or terminating an annuity contract prematurely. There is no industry standard for surrender charges, that is, each annuity product has its own unique surrender charge schedule. The charge is usually expressed as a percentage of the amount withdrawn prematurely from the contract. The percentage tends to decline over time, ultimately becoming zero.

TRADITIONAL IRA – See IRA (Individual Retirement Account)

TERM END POINT – Crediting methods measuring index movements over a greater timeframe than a year or two. The opposite of an annual reset method. Also referred to as a term point-to-point method. Say that the index value was at 100 on the first day of the period. If the calculated index value was at 150 at the end of the period the positive index movement would be 50 percent (150-100/100). The company would credit a percentage of this movement as excess interest. Index movement is calculated and interest credited at the end of the term and interim movements during the period are ignored.

TERM HIGH POINT (HIGH WATER MARK) – A type of term end point structure that uses the highest anniversary index level as the end point. Say that the index value was at 100 on the first day of the period, reached a value of 160 at the end of a contract year during the period, and ended the period at 150. A term high point method would use the 160 value – the highest contract anniversary point reached during the period, as the end point and the gross index gain would be 60 percent (160-100/100). The company would then apply a participation rate to the gain.

TERM YIELD SPREAD – A type of term end point structure which calculates the total index gain for a period, computes the annual compound rate of return deducts a yield spread from the annual rate of return and then recalculates the total index gain for the period based on the net annual rate. Say that an index increased from 100 to 200 by the end of a nine year period. This is the equivalent of an 8 percent compound annual interest rate. If the annuity had a 2 percent term yield spread this would be deducted from the annual interest rate (8 percent-2 percent) and the net rate would be credited to the contract (6 percent) for each of the nine years. Total index gain may also be computed by using the highest anniversary index level as the end point.

VARIABLE ANNUITY – A contract issued by an insurance company offering separate accounts invested in a wide variety of stocks and/or bonds. The investment risk is borne by the annuity owner. Variable annuities are considered securities and require appropriate securities registration.

1035 EXCHANGE – The 1035 exchange refers to the section of tax code that allows annuity owners the flexibility to exchange one annuity for another without incurring any immediate tax liabilities. This action is most often utilized when an annuity holder decides they want to upgrade an annuity to a more favorable one, but they do not want to activate unnecessary tax liabilities that would typically be encountered when surrendering an existing annuity contract.

401(K) ROLLOVER – See IRA Rollover

Made in the USA
Columbia, SC
12 October 2020

22642335R00114